Mundane Reasoning by
Parallel Constraint Satisfaction

Mark Derthick
MCC
Austin, Texas

Mundane Reasoning by Parallel Constraint Satisfaction

Pitman, London

Morgan Kaufmann Publishers, Inc., San Mateo, California

PITMAN PUBLISHING
128 Long Acre, London WC2E 9AN

A Division of Longman Group UK Limited

© Mark Derthick 1990

First published 1990

Available in the Western Hemisphere from
MORGAN KAUFMANN PUBLISHERS, INC.,
2929 Campus Drive, San Mateo, California 94402

ISSN 0268-7526

British Library Cataloguing in Publication Data

Derthick, Mark
    Mundane reasoning by parallel constraint satisfaction.—
(Research notes in artificial intelligence,
ISSN 0268-7526).
    1. Artificial intelligence. Applications of human
reasoning
    I. Title   II. Series
    006.3

    ISBN 0-273-08833-5

Library of Congress Cataloging in Publication Data

Derthick, Mark.
    Mundane reasoning by parallel constraint satisfaction / Mark
Derthick.
    p.   cm.—(Research notes in artificial intelligence,
ISSN 0268-7526)
    ISBN 1-55860-133-3
    1. Parallel processing (Electronic computers).   2. Artificial
intelligence.   3. Reasoning.   I. Title.   II. Series.
QA76.5.D434   1990
006.3—dc20

Reproduced and printed by photolithography
in Great Britain by Biddles Ltd, Guildford

Contents

Abstract

Connectionist networks are well suited to everyday common sense reasoning. Their ability to simultaneously satisfy multiple soft constraints allows them to select from conflicting information in finding a plausible interpretation of a situation. However these networks are poor at reasoning using the standard semantics of classical logic, based on truth in all possible models. This thesis shows that using an alternate semantics, based on truth in a single most plausible model, there is an elegant mapping from theories expressed using the syntax of propositional logic onto connectionist networks. An extension of this mapping to allow for limited use of quantifiers suffices to build a network from knowledge bases expressed in a frame language similar to KL-ONE. Although finding optimal models of these theories is intractable, the networks admit a fast hill climbing search algorithm that can be tuned to give satisfactory answers in familiar situations. The Role Shift problem illustrates the potential of this approach to harmonize conflicting information, using structured distributed representations. Although this example works well, much remains before realistic domains are feasible.

Acknowledgments

This work was carried out in the School of Computer Science, nee CSD, at Carnegie-Mellon University. I am indebted (or rather *not* indebted due) to the Office of Naval Research for four years of support from a Graduate Research Fellowship. The most rewarding aspect of my graduate studies was the warmth and encouragement of the research community. The developers of KL-ONE and related frame based languages have patiently answered my questions and let me use their systems. Several visits to the Artificial Intelligence Principles group at Bell Labs clarified my understanding of hybrid representation systems. Conferences and workshops are what makes a field a community, and I am grateful to the organizers of the Cognitive Science conference, the CMU Connectionist Summer Schools, and the NMSU High-Level Connectionist workshop.

The Boltzmann research group at CMU was a constant source of ideas. David Ackley wrote the code, in his uniquely colorful style, that has evolved into μKLONE. Barak Pearlmutter and Richard Szeliski were my math experts. Oren Etzioni, David Plaut, and Roni Rosenfeld provided philosophical critiques over many a dining table. Jon Doyle, Warren Goldfarb, and Jeff Horty helped with a disjoint set of philosophical questions—the logical ones that have answers. Mark Day forced me out from behind some of my protective jargon, at least in the first chapter of this thesis.

My committee took an active role in guiding the research towards attainable, worthwhile goals. Jay McClelland turned what might have been a confining un-exceptional semantics toward the problems of inconsistency and common sense situations. Ron Brachman kept me straight about what advantages connectionist systems could rightly claim, and provided copious suggestions for improving the form and content of the thesis. Geoff Hinton and Dave Touretzky deserve much of the credit for the design decisions, large and small, that went into μKLONE. Both devoted countless hours discussing technical questions, and patiently improving my technical writing.

Most of all I thank Geoff Hinton for introducing me to research and sharing his enthusiasm and ideas. I will never forget that for one Saturday afternoon I believed I was a witness to the solution of the AI problem. One such glimpse is enough to sustain a career. I have been coached by giants. If I have not yet stood on their shoulders, we have already held hands.

for all the reasonable people

1 Introduction

1.1 Mundane Reasoning

Mundane reasoning is the process of making the kind of unconscious decisions people constantly make every day: which chair to sit in, what a word means, how to categorize an object given its properties. It constitutes what others have called "the micro-structure of cognition" [Rumelhart *et al.*, 1986b] or "subcognition" [Hofstadter, 1985]. Categorization may require recalling earlier instances and consideration of the current context, in addition to general knowledge about the category. Yet people perform this task automatically and quickly. This ability must at least reflect expertise in retrieving relevant accumulated experience from a vastly larger store. Schank [1982] calls this *reminding*, and considers it to be a fundamental ingredient of intelligence. Other mundane tasks appear to have this same characteristic. Acquiring the ability to interpret complex stimuli quickly requires extensive familiarity with the domain. The term "mundane reasoning" indicates both that it is commonplace and that it must be grounded in experience of the world.

1.2 Theories of Reasoning

A competence theory describes a class of problems and their solutions. Such theories are also called "knowledge level" [Newell, 1982] or normative theories. In contrast are theories that take into account practical limitations on rationality and computability, and explain how a real agent will carry out a task. These are called performance or "symbol level" [Newell, 1982] theories. The field of artificial intelligence subsumes both the explanation of intelligence and the building of agents, and thus it needs both kinds of theories.

Because they idealize away from practical problems, competence theories are likely to be more perspicuous. Often a performance theory is derived from a competence theory by adding a process model that would implement the competence theory correctly, except for some resource limitations that must be imposed. Although it is difficult to characterize the performance of the resource-limited system independently of the process model, the loose relationship to the competence theory is still an important source of intuition. This thesis uses a combination of a competence theory and a resource-limited process model in just this way. The rest of this section reviews the background of the competence theory used, and discusses psychological evidence for a kind of process model that allows an effective implementation.

1.2.1 Frames as Competence Theories

One of the goals of knowledge representation (KR) is to find formal languages for writing down facts that are powerful enough that the desired consequences of those facts may be derived automatically. If the system can take care of manipulating the facts in appropriate ways, the facts play a more important role than those in a simple database; they constitute *knowledge*. There can certainly be programs that perform difficult tasks and have no separation between knowledge and rules for manipulating it, but in AI terminology such a program does not *represent* the knowledge it embodies. It is often the case that a system composed of a few inference rules and a lot of declarative knowledge makes intuitively good sense. Such a system can also be very powerful because of the combinatorial number of ways that facts can be combined using rules. An equally powerful system in which the facts are not separated from how they are used is likely to be impenetrably complex.

There is also a question of space efficiency. In the limit of context dependence, where a fact only is used in a single situation, the system is a lookup table. For problems as rich as natural language understanding this just is not an alternative—there are many more possible sentences than can possibly be stored. Any mundane reasoning system must make some use of rules, at least in the weak sense of combining some kind of data.

Many artificial intelligence application programs organize the knowledge they contain as frames [Minsky, 1975]. A frame describes a single concept and its properties. The

2

properties are expressed in terms of restrictions on conceptual constituents, with each constituent thought of as filling a *slot* of the frame. The BIRTHDAY-PARTY frame may, for example, contain a slot for the kind of food served, which is filled by CAKE. The HOST slot may be filled by the name of the person whose birthday it is, and the PARTICIPANTS slot is filled by a small number of children, who must be friends of the host. The restrictions on the slot fillers can represent knowledge of various sorts. For example, restrictions can specify a particular item, as in the case of the cake, or a type restriction as in the case of the host being a person. There can also be relations imposed among fillers of various slots, as in the case of the friendship requirement between host and participants. CAKE and PERSON in turn name other frames, so a knowledge base (KB) is a network of connected frames. There is also a special relationship, ISA, between frames indicating that one is more specific than the other. For instance a BIRTHDAY-PARTY ISA kind of PARTY, so knowledge about parties in general applies to birthday parties. The fact that the participants must be friends of the host applies to all parties, and this knowledge does not have to be repeated for birthday parties. In this case, BIRTHDAY-PARTY would be said to *inherit* that knowledge.

The expressive power of frame systems is the result of the abstract nature of frames. The fact that the participants at a party must be friends of the host is a concise statement that applies to all parties, including all birthday parties, including the birthday parties of all individuals the system knows about, and all the friends of all those individuals. This is an example of a rule, which can apply to innumerable specific situations. Some frame languages, including the one used in this thesis, can specify sufficiently powerful rules that deciding whether a conclusion is a necessary consequence of a KB is NP-hard. NP-hard problems are termed *intractable*, because it is unlikely that any polynomial time algorithm exists for deciding them [Garey and Johnson, 1979].

1.2.2   Semantically Based Performance Theories

Psychological experiments indicate that the inference rules people use are not very general. Even in domains where simple rules suffice to exactly capture the structure, people make errors. For instance Tversky and Kahneman [1982] have shown that in some con-

3

texts people assign higher probability to a statement of the form $a \wedge b$ than to a alone. They hypothesize that this may be due to making judgments based on representativeness rather than probability: people seem to reason by judging how well an exemplar fits a category, and by retrieving exemplars of a category, rather than by using abstract rules. Johnson-Laird [1983] has shown that people tend to draw false conclusions from syllogisms. Given the statements that "All of the bankers are athletes", and "None of the councillors are bankers" they are more likely to conclude, incorrectly, that "None of the councillors are athletes" than the correct answer, "Some of the athletes are not councillors."

Whether people perform correctly in these kinds of experiments is highly dependent on the semantics of the terms used in the problems. It seems that people cannot help but draw upon world knowledge even when the task is explicitly formal. Johnson-Laird's theory of how people reason is that they construct mental models of the situation and draw conclusions based on what is true in the model. For instance they may build a model of the first premise in which there are two bankers (both of whom are athletes), and one other athlete who is not a banker. The second premise suggests adding some councillors, say two. The resulting model is then examined and a conclusion drawn. If the two councillors are disjoint from all the athletes, the subject may respond that "none of the councillors are athletes," even though this is not true in all possible models. For instance the athlete who is not a banker could have been a councillor.

These tasks are examples in which there seems to be a plausible competence theory, yet peoples' actual performance is not explained by it. I maintain that it would be much better to follow the competence theory, but that for mundane reasoning any competence theory will be intractable. Model-based reasoning is a technique for doing mundane reasoning that admits tractable heuristic algorithms. There are three reasons that failing to correctly follow the competence theory may not be too bad.

First, in the usual semantics for KR systems, a proposition is believed only if it holds in all possible models. If the system does not have enough knowledge to eliminate models with conflicting conclusions, it would report that no conclusion is certain. In mundane domains it may be better to guess and occasionally be wrong than to believe nothing.

4

Decision theory is a widely used framework for making good guesses in economics. Although it requires examining all possible models to make optimal guesses, one commonly used heuristic in decision theory, Maximum Likelihood estimation,[1] has the same motivation as the one used here: to guess based on the most likely model. Pearl [1987a] discusses when this approach is likely to be useful in AI.

Second, if the system has built up a large KB, the facts may rule out all but a handful of possible models, in which case basing conclusions on a single model will often give the same result as checking all models. If this is not the case for some particular query, and the error that results is detected, new facts can be added to the KB to cover this situation. Eventually enough facts will have been added so that in the familiar kinds of situations that have been encountered many times before, the system will almost always find the correct answer. It would be nice to have an automatic training algorithm to do this, but there currently is none (see chapter 9).

A final justification for using an error-prone, but fast, retrieval system is if there is a supervisory reasoner to catch errors. For instance in a system for parsing natural language, Charniak [1986] uses a fast spreading activation algorithm to find related sets of concepts. Candidate sets are then evaluated by a slower reasoner that checks to see if the concepts are related in an appropriate way. In people, this conception may apply to mathematicians at work. While theorem verification must be done carefully, hypothesizing is often errorful, and seems to be beyond introspection. This is in keeping with my intuitive notion that mundane reasoning is what people do subconsciously.

Using a reasoner that has difficulty in chaining inferences and relies on redundant axioms to make up for these deficiencies, makes this approach more like ones used in low-level perceptual reasoning than most common sense reasoning (CSR) systems. Like mundane reasoning, CSR covers domains in which the rules used to describe the world are at a higher level of abstraction than the numerical laws of physics, and are general enough in scope to admit exceptions. However, CSR theories are usually concerned only with competence, and do not propose approximate algorithms (for instance [McCarthy, 1968, de Kleer and Brown, 1984]). In CSR, "model-based reasoning" usually means reasoning

---

[1]Maximum Likelihood estimation is explained in decision theory textbooks, for instance Chernoff and Moses [1959].

using a causal model of the domain [Forbus, 1984]. In this thesis, the term indicates that conclusions are drawn by searching over model theory models of the domain, rather than by using logical rules of inference. In the terminology of this thesis, causal models are actually theories since they specify constraints over possible domain states rather than the states themselves.

1.3   Overview of μKLONE

In this thesis I describe a system functionally similar to conventional frame-based KR systems, yet implemented as a model-based reasoner for efficiency. The name, μKLONE (pronounced micro-klone), indicates that it is functionally similar to KL-ONE [Brachman and Schmolze, 1985], a widely used frame system, yet is implemented in a connectionist system using *micro*-features [Hinton *et al.*, 1986]. μKLONE is not intended to be a psychological theory. I do not assert that people approximate a frame-based competence theory of retrieval, nor that the model-based implementation is the kind of implementation people are. The psychological results cited in the previous section are meant only to provide evidence that an intelligent system need not perform according to any concise formal theory.

The goal of combining frames with models is to produce an expressively powerful system with robust performance in mundane domains, in spite of incomplete and inconsistent KBs and in spite of the probable intractability of any adequate competence theory. The existing expressively powerful frame systems that have a formal semantics and complete implementation are not robust with respect to either problem. Their knowledge bases must be logically consistent, no guesses are made to remedy incomplete KBs, and they fail to return answers in a reasonable time, even for many seemingly easy queries.

Another interesting class of KR systems are based on connectionist networks. Connectionist networks were originally inspired by what is known of the structure of neural networks in the brain, and consist of many simple processors (called units), each of which communicates with many other units [Feldman and Ballard, 1982, Rumelhart *et al.*, 1986b]. They are more robust in that they can be made to always return an answer

6

quickly, and knowledge is combined evidentially, so there is no concept of inconsistency or incompleteness. However no previous connectionist implementation has had the expressive power of symbolic frame-based systems. Many connectionist systems also lack any means of specifying the KB in a high level language, independent of the mechanism (Shastri [1987] is a notable exception).

This thesis makes two principal contributions: it extends the semantics of frame-based KR languages to enhance their usefulness in mundane domains, and it describes an implementation made tractable by using heuristics that, although not formally correct, are intuitively plausible and that work well in an example domain that includes incomplete and inconsistent knowledge.

1.3.1 Knowledge Level Description

KL-ONE is a frame-based KR system originally developed by Brachman [1978], and now represented by a family of descendants, including NIKL [Vilain, 1985], LOOM [Mac Gregor and Bates, 1987], KREME [Abrett and Burstein, 1987], BACK [Nebel, 1988], Kandor [Patel-Schneider, 1984], and Krypton [Brachman *et al.*, 1983]. In these systems, frames are called *concepts* and slots are called *roles*. Knowledge is of two kinds: *Terminological* knowledge is knowledge about language, such as the fact that "square" means the same thing as "equilateral rectangle." *Assertional* knowledge is knowledge about the world, such as the fact that grass is green.

In Krypton, all terminological knowledge is grounded in a set of primitive terms. For instance if the concepts EQUILATERAL and RECTANGLE are primitive, then SQUARE can be defined as their intersection. The chief reasoning problem addressed by these systems is determining when the ISA relationship holds between frames by virtue of terminological knowledge alone (although most of them can answer questions about the world, too). This task is called classification.

The system presented here uses a similar language for defining terms, but it does not do terminological reasoning at all. The only use for non-primitive terms is as a notational convenience, similar to macros in programming languages. If a domain contains many facts about squares, it is more concise to avoid repeating "equilateral rectangle." There

7

is a front end to μKLONE that immediately expands out all definitions, so that the actual reasoning system only sees assertions, and these refer only to primitive terms.

The formal semantics of KL-ONE is specified by a mapping from statements in the language to statements in first-order logic [Schmolze, 1985]. For mundane domains, this is too inflexible. For instance it is generally true that all birds fly, but the proposition $\forall x\ bird(x) \rightarrow fly(x)$ is too strong. Penguins don't fly, dead birds don't fly, etc. It is impractical to explicitly characterize all the exceptions to the general rule and include them on the left hand side of the implication. McCarthy calls this the qualification problem [McCarthy, 1977]. Of the successors to KL-ONE, only LOOM addresses this problem, which it overcomes using default logic. μKLONE instead uses probability theory. Each assertion in the KB is given a certainty by the user, from which a complete probability distribution over models can be determined. When given a query the system returns an answer based on the most likely model (or one of the most likely models in case of a tie). In the case of consistent KBs, the most likely models are exactly those that are logically consistent with the KB. Thus except for the difference between answering based on truth in a single model, rather than truth in all possible models, μKLONE's semantics are upwardly compatible with KL-ONE's. For inconsistent KBs, where all propositions would count as valid in KL-ONE, μKLONE still can make sensible choices based on the weighted number of conflicts between the model and the theory.

1.3.2 Symbol Level Description

Implementing model-based reasoning in a connectionist network is conceptually simple and elegant. The models themselves are strict model theory models, in that they specify a domain and a truth assignment for all the predicates over that domain. (μKLONE theories have no function symbols, except for constants).

μKLONE theories always have finite models, which can therefore be specified by a finite set of ground atomic formulas. In the network, there is one unit to represent each possible such formula, so each assignment of binary states to units represents a model. Every axiom corresponds to a constraint among a subset of the units. For instance the theory $\{a,\ a \rightarrow b\}$ has a corresponding network with two units and two constraints. The unit representing the proposition *a* is constrained to be on, and the unit representing *b* is constrained to be on if unit *a* is on.

Every constraint has an associated positive weight. There is an evaluation function, called the *energy function*, that sums the weights of all the constraints that are violated by a model. In the example network, there are four possible models, situated at the corners of the unit square. The value of the function is zero for correct models of the theory, and has a higher value otherwise. The Boltzmann Machine search algorithm [Hinton and Sejnowski, 1986] can be applied to this search space. An initial model is selected, say {¬*a*, ¬*b*}. The search proceeds by randomly choosing a unit, say *a*, and deciding whether to change its state. The system compares the energy of the current model with that of the model that differs only in the state of unit *a*, that is {*a*, ¬*b*}. If the value is lower (less constraint violation), the system will usually adopt the new model as its current guess. However due to a controlled amount of randomness in the decision process, there is some chance that the old guess will be retained. If the value is higher, the system might also make the move, but with low probability. As the system is run for a long time, it moves from corner to corner, but tends to spend more of its time in low energy states. This is because the probability of leaving, and hence moving to a higher energy state, is small. By adjusting the relationship between differences in energy and probabilities of moving, the probability of being in the globally optimal state can be made to approach one arbitrarily closely as the network is run arbitrarily long. Thus given a network representing any propositional theory, this search algorithm is a provably correct way to find a model of the theory, if one exists.

In contrast, conventional KR systems such as Krypton use theorem provers to decide what is true given the assertions in the KB. There is a central controller that decides what rule to apply next, until a proof is discovered. In µKLONE the procedure-oriented theorem proving paradigm is replaced with an object-oriented, distributed one in which the constraints continually and in parallel exert pressure on the developing model to conform. Time has been traded for space. Every proof that a syntactic system could find for some proposition corresponds to some causal web of constraints in the connectionist network. Deduction is intractable for µKLONE, and having a parallel implementation is

9

of no help in the worst case. However it does make a big difference when good guesses are acceptable. In theorem provers, all possible paths are eventually searched, and there is no waste from checking the same path more than once. On the other hand, the rule application process is entirely local, and knowledge is only brought to bear when the control algorithm explicitly invokes it. If the most relevant knowledge is not invoked early, much of the search can be wasted.

In μKLONE, all knowledge is continuously brought to bear. This is somewhat wasteful in that most of it is not contributing most of the time. However by exploring all paths simultaneously, the system gradually converges on a satisfactory model, rather than suddenly going from having no evidence for a conclusion to having total certainty when a proof is found. The system designer's problem has a very different character in the two kinds of system. For intractable problems, no algorithm can work well on all problems. However some may have good average case performance. In theorem proving, good average case performance results from good search control knowledge that can pick relevant rules to invoke. In μKLONE it results from molding the topography of the evaluation function to be smooth. The evaluation that must constantly be made during search is "Is this a good answer?" rather than "Is this a good way to find the answer?"

The difficulty of incorporating variables in connectionist networks is generally seen as an important limitation. Indeed the method used here to embed theories involving quantified variables in a network is to first eliminate the variables by expanding the quantifiers into conjunctions or disjunctions over the entire domain. Although this is theoretically possible since μKLONE theories have the finite model property, the resulting propositional theory is exponentially large.

In order to produce a tractable implementation, therefore, μKLONE takes several more shortcuts, most of which widen the gap between competence and performance. Most of the work in building μKLONE dealt with making sure these shortcuts were heuristically adequate. The most interesting limitation is truncating the search space so that only propositions directly related to the subject of a query are represented by units. Others include limiting the number of Skolem functions, using a faster, deterministic search algorithm that is not guaranteed to be correct, and modifying the constraints so

10

that the energy function is smoother and more conducive to hill climbing.

The motivation for these heuristic approximations is the hope that allowing the system the freedom to guess and be wrong in some cases, rather than not return an answer, will result in a closer correspondence between what is hard for the system and what looks hard to a human. Some of the advantage of having a formal competence theory is lost if the actual system does not follow it. However, by thinking of the tractable system as an approximation to the larger provably correct one, the relation to a formal theory of reasoning is much more clear than it has been for related connectionist KR systems, such as [Hinton, 1981, McClelland and Kawamoto, 1986, Touretzky and Geva, 1987, Rumelhart, 1986, Hinton, 1986]. More of the ability to reason about structured knowledge has been retained than for any previous connectionist KR system.

1.4   The Role Shift Problem

The Role Shift problem demonstrates μKLONE's ability to slip between similar roles, using a knowledge base that describes the well known business and sports personality, Ted Turner. Imagine walking along a pier and meeting Ted, who is dressed as a sailor. Ted launches into an excited monolog on the influence of independent television stations on TV programming. It seems reasonable to conclude that Ted is a professional sailor, and that he is interested in television. If later it is discovered that Ted is a self-made millionaire playboy, the previous conclusions about Ted would probably be changed. While self-made millionaire playboys generally have jobs, they are unlikely to be involved in manual labor. Millionaire playboys often have ostentatious pastimes, so perhaps sailing is Ted's hobby rather than his job. Given that he probably has some job, the fact that he is interested in television suggests that that field may be his profession.

μKLONE can reason about such belief-revision situations. The original beliefs about Ted are encoded in a μKLONE KB, which is then compiled into a connectionist network. When this network is queried "If Ted were a self-made-millionaire-playboy, what would his job and hobby be?" it must try to reconcile being a millionaire playboy with its previous beliefs about Ted, that he is a professional sailor and is interested in tele-

11

vision. Although there are no zero energy models that agree both with the KB and the presupposition of the query, the system can still find a compromise model in which Ted is a millionaire playboy whose job is TV-Network-Management and whose hobby is Sailing, but in which he is not a professional sailor. The plausible substitution that sailing is Ted's job rather than his hobby is made because. HAS-JOB and HAS-HOBBY are both subsumed by HAS-INTEREST, making it relatively easy to slip between them. TV-Network-Management is selected as his job because it simultaneously satisfies both the constraint that self-made millionaire playboys have jobs and the constraint that Ted has an interest related to television.

A key to the success of the similarity-based matching is that terms are represented as sets of features. Hinton [1981] calls this a *distributed representation*. In this case, HAS-JOB and HAS-HOBBY share the features of their common ancestor, HAS-INTEREST.

The Role Shift problem involves knowledge that, if expressed in first-order logic, would be incomplete and inconsistent. That is, there are some propositions, p, such that neither p nor $\neg p$ is provable from the KB assertions, and other propositions such that both p and $\neg p$ are provable. An example of the latter is the proposition $has\text{-}job(Ted, Sailing)$, and an example of the former is $has\text{-}job(Ted, TV\text{-}Network\text{-}Management)$. Within logic, the problem of discarding beliefs in the face of conflicting knowledge is called counterfactual reasoning, and the problem of assuming knowledge to explain beliefs is called abductive reasoning. Using probability, both types of reasoning are subsumed by the problem of finding the most probable model.

1.5   Outline of Thesis

Chapter 2 describes a numerical semantics that can be applied to any theory expressed using the syntax of propositional logic. This semantics is designed to be as discriminating as possible in denoting a set of plausible models. Finding a plausible model given this numerically based semantics is a function optimization problem, and is provably intractable. Chapter 3 describes several connectionist and network based algorithms for finding optimal models, including the one μKLONE uses. They use hill climbing as a

12

heuristic for quickly finding good, but not necessarily optimal, models.

Chapter 4 introduces the syntax used in μKLONE, and compares its expressive power to that of full first-order logic and to the KL-ONE family of knowledge representation systems. Chapter 5 describes an idealized, but impractical implementation of μKLONE. This imaginary architecture would take the model-based approach to its extreme, in which the system literally searches over models of the KB, and uses no other data structures. This chapter uses as an example the analysis of a full adder circuit, which is hardly a mundane domain. The domain has the advantage of being well defined and easily understood, and so provides a good illustration of how the frame language is used. Second, the difficulties that the approximate architecture has with problems involving chains of inference clarify the trade-off μKLONE makes between the range of problems it can handle and the speed of reasoning. Chapter 6 describes the way the idealized architecture is modified to produce a tractable, but approximate reasoning system. A more suitable domain is used as an example, in which distributed representations produce an interesting shift between similar roles in the context of a counterfactual reasoning problem. Chapter 7 compares μKLONE with several other connectionist knowledge representation systems.

Chapter 8, "Open Questions," is where both reader and writer are free from worrying about systems and details and understanding, and can just wonder. Some questions addressed there are: Could non-symbolic representations enhance the functional power of μKLONE? Could they reduce the space complexity of the architecture? Can superposition of models explain prototype effects? How well can μKLONE handle language understanding?

The conclusion assesses the significance of μKLONE, in terms of contributions to connectionist search procedures, model based reasoning, and approximate reasoning. The need for embedding in a sequential reasoner, and the prospects for practical application are discussed.

Notably absent is a chapter called "Related Work." μKLONE combines ideas from many different systems, but there are none that share a majority of its world view. Hence references to other systems are scattered about in the sections where they are relevant. Chapter 2 discusses approaches to combining evidence and making decisions; chapter 3 describes graph-based algorithms for deriving probabilities and maximum likelihood models; chapter 4 compares μKLONE to knowledge representation systems with similar languages; and chapter 7 discusses knowledge representation systems with connectionist implementations.

2 Defining Plausible Models

This chapter and the next are intended to describe in a general way the knowledge level semantics of μKLONE and how this formal specification is heuristically implemented in a connectionist net. Putting off discussion of the actual syntax used to specify KBs until chapter 4, this chapter describes a semantics that can be applied to any theory expressed using the standard syntax of propositional logic. Similarly, the kind of connectionist network described in chapter 3 can be used to answer queries about any such theory. It is possible to think of these two chapters as specifying a very general theory of common sense reasoning, and to think of μKLONE as a particular instance of this theory.

The goal of mundane reasoning is to find a plausible interpretation of the current situation quickly. In order to allow answering as quickly as possible, a mundane reasoner is not required to add helpful information about alternative interpretations or point out unknown facts that would increase the confidence in a conclusion. On the other hand the license the mundane reasoner has to guide behavior based only on a single model puts a heavy burden on the semantics for combining the information that *is* available, so that the interpretation chosen really is the best possible.

Given a query about some knowledge base, μKLONE's semantics specify a set of most plausible models, from which one is chosen randomly and used to answer queries. Although in logic-based systems, queries are usually answered based on truth in all the models of a theory rather than just a single model, μKLONE can be compared to other logics in terms of the set of models allowed by a given theory. This chapter compares in a very general way the logic of μKLONE with classical logic, with Reiter's default logic [Reiter, 1980], and with NETL [Fahlman, 1979], all of which have been used for knowledge representation. The conclusion is that even though the final semantic interpretation of a query is a function from models to binary truth values, there are advantages to using numbers in intermediate interpretations of knowledge bases. The next chapter discusses implementations, and suggests additional advantages of using numbers instead of truth

15

values for efficient searching. Expert systems such as MYCIN and Prospector also use numbers when reasoning, for both the knowledge level and symbol level advantages. A brief comparison with the latter is also given.

2.1   Classical Logic

In classical logic, a model is a $<D, I>$ tuple, where D is a set of individuals, or *domain*, and I is an interpretation function that specifies the extension of each predicate and function symbol. A theory is a set of sentences, or axioms. A model is said to be a model of a theory if all the axioms are true when the quantifiers range over D and the predicates and functions are given the interpretation I. To put this into common terms with μKLONE, the models of a consistent classical theory are its most plausible models. It is convenient to refer to the most plausible models of μKLONE theories as the models of the theory as well, even though they are in general not consistent with all the axioms. The phrase "models consistent with the theory" is reserved for the classical meaning of "model of the theory."

The power of classical logic is the relationship between proof theory and model theory. There are proof systems that are sound and complete; that is, there are sets of rules of inference such that any sentence derived using these rules will be true in all consistent models, and any sentence true in all consistent models has a proof using these rules. A proof is a finite sequence of steps, each of which can be checked by examining only a small amount of information. Yet it guarantees the truth of a sentence in what may be an infinite number of models.

KL-ONE reasons according to the principles of classical logic. A knowledge base has a straightforward translation into logical axioms, and the system believes any sentence that it can prove from these axioms using the standard rules of inference. The main problem with classical logic for knowledge representation is that many useful generalizations about the world admit exceptions. For instance we want to be able to say "birds fly," even though this is not universally true. It is simply impractical to list all the possible exceptions to the rule. If the rule is encoded as $\forall x(bird(x) \rightarrow fly(x))$, and it is known

16

that Tweety is a bird that doesn't fly, the theory is inconsistent. Given an inconsistent KB, classical logic specifies an empty set of models. For a mundane reasoner that must make some guess, this is of no help.

2.2   Default Logic

In default logic much effort is made to ensure that the set of most plausible models is "reasonable," neither empty nor so large that it includes counter-intuitive interpretations. In Reiter's default logic [Reiter, 1980], a KB consists of both axioms and default rules. Axioms are the same as in classical logic. An example of a default rule is

$$\frac{bird(x) \ : \ M \ fly(x)}{fly(x)}$$

This rule means "if x is a bird, and it is consistent to believe that x flies, then conclude that x flies." Reading left-to-right and top-to-bottom, the three parts of a default rule are called the *prerequisite*, the *justification*, and the *consequent*. In default logic, determining the most plausible models requires an intermediate step. First a set of *extensions* is found. An extension is a minimal superset of the axioms closed under the standard rules of inference, and containing in addition the consequent of each default rule whose prerequisite is contained in that set and whose justification is not inconsistent with that set. The models of a default theory include all the models of all the extensions.

The key to the improved discriminability of default logic is that it uses a global measure over the entire KB in deciding what to believe. In classical logic, the fact that a proof does not depend on all that is known makes reasoning elegant, but insufficiently flexible. With the default rule above, and in the absence of any other information, if Tweety is a bird, then the system will believe that Tweety flies. But if there are axioms stating that Tweety is a penguin, and that penguins do not fly, then the system will believe that Tweety is a bird, but does not fly.

Sometimes there are conflicting default rules. For instance if the rule that penguins do not fly is made a default rule instead of an axiom, there are two different extensions. In one Tweety flies because he is a bird, and in the other Tweety does not fly because he is a penguin. Since penguins are kinds of birds, the default rule about penguins is

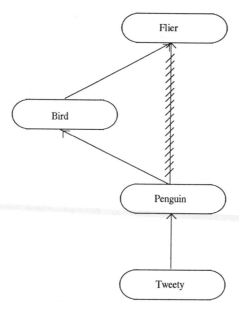

Figure 2.1: An example inheritance problem using NETL's notation.

more specific and should override the default about birds. In normal default theories,[1] adding defaults can never eliminate an extension [Reiter, 1980], so each default rule must explicitly mention situations in which it is to be overridden [Touretzky, 1986b]. This makes defeasible assertions just as verbose as in classical logic.

2.3 NETL

NETL [Fahlman, 1979] uses network-based algorithms to determine class inclusion relationships. Figure 2.1 shows how the above example involving conflicting defaults is expressed in NETL. The set of most plausible models includes only the one where Tweety does not fly, because of the *shortest path heuristic*: the negative path from Penguin to Flier is shorter than the positive path through Bird.

In this case at least, the heuristic succeeds in picking the extension that is intuitively

---

[1] In normal default theories, the justification of every default rule is identical to the consequent. This is an extremely useful special case: Reiter has said "I know of no naturally occurring default which cannot be represented in this form." Morris [1988] has suggested that anomalous extensions can be eliminated through the use of non-normal defaults, but there is as yet no method for solving this problem without explicitly linking the exception to the rule it pre-empts.

correct. Touretzky [1986b] shows that this heuristic fails for some networks containing redundant links, and has proposed a more sophisticated one called *inferential distance*. Using it, the default about penguins defeats the default about birds because bird can be inferred from penguin, but not vice versa. More recent work has shown that intuitions about more complicated nets sometimes are not so clear as to which model is correct, and that there are network algorithms corresponding to several plausible strategies [Touretzky *et al.*, 1987].

2.4 ϵ Semantics

Graph based algorithms examined by Horty, Thomason, and Touretzky [Horty and Thomason, 1987, Horty *et al.*, 1987] give stronger results than default logic, and are designed to match intuitions on a catalog of standard examples, such as the one about Tweety. They are justified by their behavior on these problems and by the intuitiveness of the algorithms, rather than on *a priori* semantic grounds. Pearl [1987b] has proposed a semantic foundation based on probability theory for these networks. The link from bird to flier is interpreted as an assertion that the conditional probability of flying given that one is a bird is $1 - \epsilon$. A conclusion is sanctioned if for all $\epsilon > 0$, and all probability distributions satisfying the default assertions imposed by the network, its probability is at least $1 - O(\epsilon)$.

In the Tweety case, the correct conclusion, that Tweety doesn't fly, follows. However using solely the procedure above, adding restrictions can only reduce the number of distributions considered, so all inferences are monotonic. Pearl gets nonmonotonicity by adding conditional independence assumptions. For instance, the theory {*robin* → *bird, bird* → *flier*} does not sanction the conclusion that robins are fliers, because in some probability distributions, where robins are exceptional birds, few robins fly. Pearl eliminates such exceptional distributions from consideration by considering only those that are *Markov fields* relative to the inheritance graph:

Definition:[2] P is said to be a Markov field relative to Γ iff whenever Z is a

---

[2][Pearl, 1987b]

set of vertices (predicates) separating p from q in Γ then

$$P(q|p, Z) = P(q|Z)$$

Since $Z = bird$ separates robin from flier, only distributions where $P(flier|robin, bird) = P(flier|bird) = 1 - \epsilon$ are considered, so robins fly. If a link is added saying robins aren't fliers, making the theory isomorphic to the penguin case, more distributions meet the Markov condition, and the conclusion is defeated.

The resulting system still does not sanction as many conclusions as graph algorithms in the case of positive conjunctions. If both Quakers and Republicans tend to be registered voters, the graph algorithms will conclude someone who is both a Quaker and a Republican is a registered voter. However individuals in the intersection of two classes may be exceptions with respect to both classes: though both Quakers and Republicans may tend to be ideological extremists, people who are both may be ideological centrists. Since this kind of case is rare, Pearl adds another condition on the distributions considered to eliminate it: If u's are by default w's, and v's are by default w's, then things that are both u's and v's are by default w's. The independence assumptions and the positive conjunction principle, like the graph-based algorithms, are reasonable yet *ad hoc* rules. At least with ϵ semantics fewer of these rules are required.

2.5 Certainties

Although the inferential distance heuristic is useful in that it eliminates some spurious extensions, it is only applicable in situations expressible in network notation. Rigorous analysis has only been applied to acyclic networks whose nodes represent one-place predicates. In the future it may be possible to extend the formal analysis to handle properties (two-place predicates), as was done informally in NETL. Also, John Horty [1988] is examining the extension of the inferential distance ordering to apply to any default logic theory. Even if these efforts succeed, there will still be ambiguous theories such as the Nixon diamond. In this theory, Quakers tend to be Pacifists, Republicans tend not to be Pacifists, and Dick is both a Quaker and a Republican. There are no topological clues as to which of the conflicting defaults should prevail; yet if the relative strengths are known, there ought to be a concise way to incorporate it into the KB.

One way to further restrict the set of extensions is to define a partial order over them (called the *better-world* predicate in [Ginsberg, 1986]) and consider only its maximal extensions. If *better-world* is specified by enumeration, the resulting KB will be as verbose as if exceptions are mentioned explicitly in the default rules. In order to make all pairs of extensions comparable, a KB of size $O(n)$ will have to be augmented by a preference specification of size $O(2^n)$.

If *better-world*(E_1, E_2) can be specified in terms of some existing predicate and some function defined over extensions, *better-world*$(E_1, E_2) \equiv p(f(E_1), f(E_2))$, then the augmented theory may be much more compact. In μKLONE f is a cost function called the *energy function* and p is arithmetic $<$. f counts up the (weighted) number of axioms that fail to hold. This method limits the range of orderings that can be specified, but only linear space is required and the ordering that results is total.

The axioms are ordinary sentences, with no prerequisite. They are interpreted as "If p can be assumed, do so." This corresponds to normal defaults with no prerequisite, so the theories expressible are a strict subset of default logic theories. The default logic translation of the assertion about birds is therefore

$$\frac{: \; M \; bird(x) \to fly(x)}{bird(x) \to fly(x)}$$

Since the step from bird to flies is now an (defeasible) implication rather than an inference rule, its contrapositive can be used to derive $\neg bird(Tweety)$ from $\neg flies(Tweety)$.[3] This backwards use of links is never done in graph algorithms. Intuition does not provide a clear preference for either scheme. In some cases one might want to conclude of an individual that does not fly that it is not a bird.

The numbers attached to axioms are called *certainties* because their function is analogous to the numbers attached to rules in MYCIN [Shortliffe, 1976], Prospector [Duda *et al.*, 1979], and other expert systems. "Certainty" is a generic term, since different systems have different calculi for deriving the certainty of a conclusion from the certainties of its justifications. MYCIN's combination rules are based on confirmation theory [Carnap,

---

[3] Thanks to Kurt Konolige for pointing this out.

1950] and Prospector's are based on probability theory. μKLONE's certainty calculus is particularly simple. Certainties are derived only for complete models, so the difficulties associated with propagating probabilities through long derivations are avoided.

2.6 μKLONE

To a first approximation, the energy of a model is the number of axioms violated, weighted by their certainty. However if the KB asserts that the friends of people must be people, then it seems that John is a worse example of a person if his friends include his dog and his cat than if he is only friends with his dog.[4] Yet in both cases only a single axiom is violated. To prevent one wrong from justifying another, universally quantified assertions are treated as conjunctions of many separate assertions, each about particular individuals, and each having the same certainty as the original quantified assertion.

There are a number of schemes for capturing the meaning of propositional formulas in arithmetic expressions. In Boolean algebra with positive logic, where 1 represents true and 0 false, AND corresponds to min, OR to max, and NOT to $1-x$. In fuzzy logic the same functions are used, but the domain is expanded to the continuous interval between zero and one, rather than only the endpoints [Zadeh, 1986]. The truth value of an expression is meant to capture the likelihood of the whole as a function of the likelihoods of its composants.

The goal of μKLONE is very different. It does not need the exact likelihood of a formula being true, but only an ordering over models. This gives it the flexibility to use numbers outside the range [0, 1]. These numbers are proportional to log probabilities, so they do in fact determine the probabilities of formulas. However a normalization step is required to find the proportionality constant, so it is impossible to compute the probability of a formula strictly from the probabilities of its constituents. Therefore this scheme is unsuitable for syntactic reasoning, as is usually done in fuzzy logic and expert systems. The ability to use numbers in the interval $< 0, \infty >$ in model-based reasoning gives it more power to discriminate between models, as the following example shows. In

---

[4]Up to a point. In the actual implementation the total penalty for John's broadmindedness reaches an asymptote as the number of non-human friends increases.

boolean algebra or fuzzy logic, the sentences "Lincoln was buried in Grant's tomb" and "Lincoln was buried in Grant's tomb and violets are green" have the same likelihood, yet they impose different orderings on possible models. A KB containing the second sentence will rank the actual world lower than a KB containing only the first, because the actual world violates two constraints rather than just one.

A second difference between μKLONE and most other schemes is the polarity of the mapping between truth values and numbers. In Boolean algebra, positive logic is conventional, but negative logic could equally well be used. In this case true is zero, false is one, AND is max, and OR is min. For μKLONE, which counts constraint violation, it is crucial that zero constraint violation correspond to true. If the KB contains the single assertion p, the energy of models in which p fails to hold should be increased. The constraint expressing this is (ON p). The energy equation is $E^\alpha = s_p^\alpha$ where s_p^α is zero if p is true in model α and one otherwise. For convenience the distinction between the variable p and the state, s_p, of the unit representing the variable is dropped, as is the superscript indicating the model. The constraint (ON p) is also usually written simply p.

Like the negative logic version of Boolean algebra, μKLONE translates OR as min and NOT as $1 - x$. However to be able to distinguish pairs of sentences like the ones about Lincoln, it translates AND as $+$ rather than max. The correct way to think about this is that models that violate multiple conjuncts of an assertion have a higher constraint violation. Being sloppy, it is also possible to think of the propositions themselves as having truth values that range from true to false to extra false. On this view, ANDing two false propositions results in a proposition that is even more false. A problem now arises with NOT when it is applied to these extra false propositions. If proposition p has energy 2, then (NOT p) has energy $1 - 2 = \ 1$, which is outside the domain of plausibilities. Therefore a syntactic restriction is imposed on the language that NOT can never be applied to a proposition whose plausibility can be anything other than zero or one. Thus only disjunctions and other negations can appear inside the scope of a negation sign.[5] In logic, it is always possible to use de Morgan's laws to push in negation signs so they only apply to atoms, and this can at most double the size of the formula.

---

[5]Table A.1 gives a grammar that incorporates the syntactic restrictions.

Certainty	Axiom
50	$\forall x\ bird(x) \rightarrow flier(x)$
100	$\forall x\ penguin(x) \rightarrow bird(x)$
80	$\forall x\ penguin(x) \rightarrow \neg flier(x)$
80	$penguin(Tweety)$

Expanding the quantifiers over the domain $\{Tweety, Opus\}$ gives:

Certainty	Axiom
50	$bird(Tweety) \rightarrow flier(Tweety)$
50	$bird(Opus) \rightarrow flier(Opus)$
100	$penguin(Tweety) \rightarrow bird(Tweety)$
100	$penguin(Opus) \rightarrow bird(Opus)$
80	$penguin(Tweety) \rightarrow \neg flier(Tweety)$
80	$penguin(Opus) \rightarrow \neg flier(Opus)$
80	$penguin(Tweety)$

Figure 2.2: The encoding of the Tweety problem using the language of FOL augmented with certainties (top) can be written in a canonical propositional form to be used to calculate the energy of a model, once the model's domain (here $\{Tweety, Opus\}$) is known (bottom).

These constraints enable any propositional theory to be expressed as an energy function. To build in the formula $a \wedge (\neg b \vee c)$ requires an AND constraint with two components, an ON constraint and an OR constraint, which in turn has two components. If a, b, and c represent the state of the three units representing the atomic propositions, the energy function for the complete network is

$$E = a + \min((1-b), c)$$

A final constraint type is required to adjust the certainty of constraints. WITH-WEIGHT multiplies the energy penalty for violating a constraint by a constant, w, the weight assigned to that constraint. For instance, the energy function for (WITH-WEIGHT (ON a)) is $w \times a$. The name is "with-weight" rather than "with-certainty" because this is the traditional nomenclature in connectionist networks. In the thesis "weight" and "certainty" have the same meaning. I tend to use the former when talking about implementation issues and the latter when talking at the functional level.

Figure 2.2 shows how the Tweety example would be encoded using the syntax of

24

first-order logic augmented by certainties, and how it is re-expressed as a propositional theory for determining the cost function of models with a given domain. In contrast to NETL's shortest path heuristic, μKLONE can be thought of as using a strongest path heuristic. The strength of a path is, to first order, the certainty of its weakest link (see section 3.7.2). Associating certainties with the links in figure 2.1, the strength of the positive path from Tweety to Flier is min(80, 100, 50), and that of the negative path is min(80, 80). Thus μKLONE also concludes that Tweety does not fly, but for a different reason. If the certainty of the assertion that birds fly were raised to 100, the two paths would both have strength 80. Either the assertion that Tweety is a Penguin could be dropped, or the assertion that penguins do not fly could be dropped. Using numbers, μKLONE has more flexibility than NETL; however if NETL's heuristics correctly match intuitions this flexibility is unnecessary. For class inclusion questions, NETL and its descendants in fact do quite well.

For consistent theories, the resulting semantics is compatible with that of classical logic. The classical models will all have zero energy, and all other models will have higher energy (Appendix A proves this). For inconsistent theories, which have no classical models, there will be no zero-energy models either, but there will still be a well defined set of minimum-energy models that least violate the weighted assertions. It is usually desirable to consider only the minimal models in this set. This can be done by adding an energy penalty proportional to the size of the extensions of all the predicates. As long as this penalty is much smaller than the penalty for violating assertions, it will only prune the set, and never introduce models into the set that violate more assertions. This numerical notion of minimality is stronger than the subset notion usually used in defining minimal models, in that $\{p\, q\}$ is smaller than $\{q\, r\, s\}$ rather than incomparable.

Although these four constraint types are sufficient to define an energy function that respects the semantics of any μKLONE KB, there exist many other schemes for translating KBs into energy functions that agree on the energy to assign every model. They only disagree when the atoms are assigned truth values intermediate between zero and one. For pragmatic reasons three other constraint types, introduced in section 3.7.1, are used in μKLONE: IMPLIES, VERY, and ATLEAST.

The set of minimum-energy models of a knowledge base is unfortunately not invariant under the usual rules of logical inference. For example the meaning of $\{a, b\}$ is not the same as $\{a, a \rightarrow b\}$ because the empty model violates two axioms in the first theory, but only one in the second. Since μKLONE never performs syntactic inference anyway, this is less of a drawback than in deductive systems. Ginsberg has pointed out that this is a likely consequence of any system that does counterfactual reasoning [Ginsberg, 1986]. The counterfactual consequences for b of $\neg a$ depend on the reasons for believing b in the first place. If it is believed only because a is believed, it should no longer be believed when a no longer is.

Thus there may be some justification in considering syntactic differences when reasoning. Systems that can semantically distinguish every pair of syntactically distinct entities probably go too far, however. In μKLONE there are semantically irrelevant syntactic distinctions. Propositions that can be derived from one another strictly by using the commutative, associative, and distributive laws are equivalent semantically.

Using de Morgan's laws also changes the meaning of a formula under the above translation. The energy contribution of the assertion $A \wedge B$ is $A + B$, while that of $\neg(\neg A \vee \neg B)$ is $1 - \min(1 - A, 1 - B) = \max(A, B)$. In the model where both a and b are false, the energy contribution of the first assertion is two, while that of the second is one. The two forms correspond to different beliefs about the independence of a and b. In the first, they are statistically independent, while in the second they are positively correlated. The expert system Prospector [Duda et $al.$, 1979] uses a similar mapping of logic onto logarithms of probabilities, and explicitly has two forms of AND available for the user, one corresponding to adding the log probabilities, and one corresponding to taking their maximum.

The main difference between Prospector's semantics and μKLONE's is that Prospector uses absolute log probabilities, rather than unnormalized ones. This enables it to determine real probabilities while doing syntactic inference, but only by making conditional independence assumptions at each step. These assumptions may not be globally consistent, so the reasoning algorithm does not necessarily respect the semantics. This is put forward as a feature, because it means the algorithm works even when the knowledge engineer specifies an inconsistent probability distribution, a case that seems hard to avoid in practice.

2.7 Suppositions

There is one previous system whose goal is to find a single most plausible interpretation, and that uses numerical constraints to speed the search process. Hinton's PhD thesis [Hinton, 1977] uses linear programming to find solutions to linear inequalities representing constraints on interpretations of images of puppets composed of rectangles. As in boolean algebra and possibility theory, the supposition value of a proposition is restricted to lie between zero and one, where one means true and zero false. Thus suppositions cannot be used to distinguish among models of inconsistent theories. Unlike possibility theory, however, Hinton is wary of giving suppositions a probabilistic interpretation. He is perfectly happy with binary truth values, merely unhappy that they make it difficult to find good search heuristics for finding satisficing models.

Hinton translates $supposition(\neg p)$ as $1 - supposition(p)$, and the translation of an assertion in conjunctive normal form $(p_{11} \vee \cdots p_{1n_1}) \wedge \cdots \wedge (p_{m1} \vee \cdots \vee p_{mn_m})$ is the set of inequalities $\{p_{11} + \cdots + p_{1n_1} \geq 1, \cdots, p_{m1} + \cdots + p_{mn_m} \geq 1\}$. Although a model satisfies the CNF formula if and only if it satisfies the inequalities, there may be non-integer solutions as well. Hinton discusses techniques from the linear programming literature for finding integer solutions, although he reports that his puppet-finding system never converged to a non-integer solution. For consistent theories, Hinton seems to have found a heuristic method for finding models that is fast in the typical case.

2.8 Probability

For the purpose of specifying the set of most plausible models of a KB, there is no need to treat the energies of models as anything more than simply numbers. The problem of finding one of the most plausible models is just a problem of function optimization. However, the optimization algorithm that the idealized provably correct version of μKLONE

27

uses works by sampling from a probability distribution in which the probabilities of all but the most likely models go to zero. The next chapter describes network algorithms for probabilistic reasoning, but first the interpretation of energies as probabilities is given.

Certainties are related to probabilities using the Boltzmann Distribution [Schrödinger, 1946], which relates the energy of possible states in a physical system to their probability:

$$\frac{P(\alpha)}{P(\beta)} = e^{-(E_\alpha - E_\beta)/T} \tag{2.1}$$

Here α and β are any two states of the system and T is temperature. The log of the probability ratio between any two states is proportional to the energy difference between the states. Temperature is the constant of proportionality, and provides a degree of freedom in the mapping from energies to probabilities. At high temperatures the ratio is close to one, meaning that the probabilities are relatively insensitive to energy differences. But as the temperature approaches zero only the lowest energy models will have an appreciable probability. Given the probability ratios between all pairs of models, the probability of each model is uniquely determined.

One optimization technique described in the next chapter, simulated annealing, gets good convergence properties by gradually lowering the temperature parameter during search. Thus even though the goal is finding a minimum-energy model, the probabilistic interpretation of the energy function plays an important pragmatic role.

This probability distribution is related to the Maximum Entropy distribution, which has been advocated for use in expert systems [Konolige, 1979]. The entropy, S, of a distribution is

$$S = \sum_\alpha \Pr(\alpha) \cdot \log \Pr(\alpha)$$

where α ranges over all states of the system. This function is maximized when all states are equally probable. When the model designer has partial information about the desired probability distribution, the maximum entropy principle can still be used to pick a distribution consistent with the designers constraints. For instance if a model includes binary variables a and b, and $\Pr(a) + \Pr(b) = 0.5$, the maximum entropy distribution has $\Pr(a) = 0.25$, $\Pr(b) = 0.25$, and the other variables have probability one half, with all variables independent.

In contrast, the Boltzmann Distribution is the one that minimizes free energy

$$F(T) = <E(T)> - T \cdot S$$

Free energy optimizes a combination of average energy *and* entropy over all possible distributions, rather than optimizing entropy alone over some restricted space of distributions. If infinite energy was assigned to distributions violating the designer's constraints, and zero energy was assigned to allowed distributions, the two methods would yield the same result. In practice, it is difficult to find a set of hard constraints that is consistent. Using soft constraints, any energy function results in a consistent probability distribution. Also, it seems more natural to give the system suggestions from which it can deviate if the entropy reward is high enough, rather then absolute requirements.

3 Finding Plausible Models

3.1 Motivation

The previous chapter discussed various approaches for formal specification of the set of most plausible models of a theory. There remain alternative ways of using such a specification to answer queries. In classical logic decisions are generally based on validity. A proposition is believed if it is true in all of the most plausible models, believed false if it is false in all these models, and no decision is made in other cases. This decision rule is very conservative; you can be confident of its conclusions, but often getting a conclusion will require further work to add sufficient information to the KB. The goal of mundane reasoning is to find an answer quickly, even if the system has to guess, so validity is not a suitable decision rule.

Using probability theory, even with logically incomplete or inconsistent information, the Boltzmann Distribution can be used to specify a complete probability distribution. From this the probability of any proposition can be determined by summing the probabilities of the models in which it holds. In cases where classical logic would find the proposition true, it will have a probability of one using the zero temperature Boltzmann Distribution. In cases where logic makes no decision, the numerical probability can still be used as the basis of a decision.

This process is computationally intensive, requiring a summation over an exponential number of models. One often used heuristic is Maximum Likelihood estimation. The most probable model is found, and the truth of the proposition in that model is used to make the decision. Model based reasoning, as used in this thesis, is in fact Maximum Likelihood estimation.[1]

---

[1] μKLONE queries have presuppositions, which are combined with the prior information contained in the KB to produce a posterior distribution, and the most plausible model is a mode of this distribution. When Maximum Likelihood estimation is applied to posterior distributions, it is sometimes called Maximum a Posteriori estimation [Geman and Geman, 1984].

Finding even a single most plausible model is still a hard problem. In μKLONE, it is a generalization of the problem of finding models of boolean formulas, which is well known to be NP-complete by Cook's theorem [Garey and Johnson, 1979]. Still, model-based approaches seem to be better suited to fast heuristic algorithms than approaches based on finding derivations of an answer. Levesque has suggested simplifying the knowledge representation problem by using "vivid knowledge bases," which are essentially models [Levesque, 1986]. A vivid KB is complete, which means it has a unique model. To guarantee that the unique model is easy to compute, two constraints are imposed [Selman, 1987]: 1) there is a one-to-one correspondence between a subset of the symbols in the KB and the objects of interest in the world, and 2) For every relationship of interest in the world, there is an easily computable relationship among symbols in the KB. "Easily computable" means something like locally computable, or computable in constant time. Given an ordinary KB, it is first put in vivid form. In that form, answering queries will be simple. However, putting an incomplete KB in vivid form requires assumptions to be made, with the result that unsound inferences may result.

3.2   Stochastic Simulation

In stochastic simulation, a software model is built that mimics the behavior of the domain to the extent that the probability distribution of its states matches the distribution specified by the domain description. In order to estimate the probability of a proposition, its value must be sampled over time, just as an empirical estimate would be made from any real system. In order to get a good estimate, the system must be allowed to settle towards equilibrium (for accuracy) and then many samples must be taken (for precision). For simulated annealing, Geman and Geman [1984] show that equilibrium is reached in exponential time; in fact, stochastic simulation is a poor way to compute exact probabilities. However it offers a method of guessing, simply by not waiting very long or sampling very many times. Since μKLONE uses only one sample, the quality of the estimate is only dependent on the waiting time. This is an ideal type of approximation algorithm, because there is no need to pre-allocate a certain amount of resources. The algorithm simply runs, and when the system can wait no longer for an answer, the current estimate can be returned. The longer the system waits, the better the estimate becomes.

In stochastic simulation, state changes occur by making well-defined *moves*. From the current state, another accessible state is chosen stochastically as a possible next state. This choice must be made by sampling from the same marginal distribution over these accessible states that is exhibited by the system being modeled. Then the simulation will gradually approach an equilibrium distribution that correctly mimics the target system. Each proposition is periodically *probed*—that is, given a chance to change belief states. The possible moves are either to take on a state of true, or to take on a state of false. The marginal probability distribution of the associated proposition is calculated, conditioned on the state of all the other nodes. If the marginal probability of the proposition being true is, say, .6, then the move 'state → true' is made sixty percent of the time, and otherwise 'state → false' is made.

3.3   Bayesian Belief Networks

Pearl's work is perhaps the best known example of using graphs for probabilistic reasoning. In his Bayesian belief networks, nodes (which I will call units for compatibility with Boltzmann terminology) correspond to propositions, and a proposition p that causally depends on q is connected to q with a directed edge labeled with the conditional probability. For domains in which the resulting graph is a tree (or can be made into a tree by coalescing nodes), there are efficient algorithms for explicitly computing posterior probabilities of propositions [Pearl, 1986], as well as for computing complete models when belief commitments are wanted [Pearl, 1987a]. New information to be considered in calculating posteriors is represented by *clamping* the state of units representing known propositions to zero or one. The algorithms adjust the states only of unclamped units.[2]

When the reasoning algorithm described by Pearl [1986] is applied to a Bayesian belief network that is not a tree, it is possible to transform it into a tree, but for general graphs the size may increase exponentially. Bayesian belief networks can be treated as

---

[2]If the new information is an unconditional probability other than zero or one, extra nodes and links can be added to the network so that clamping still works.

models of the domain, however, and stochastic simulation can be used to quickly find plausible models [Henrion, 1986]. Calculating the marginal distributions conditioned on a particular proposition is easy, because it only depends on the state of neighboring propositions in the Bayesian belief network.

3.4 Simulated Annealing

Simulated annealing is a special case of stochastic simulation in which the state probabilities are specified by the Boltzmann Distribution, which has temperature as a free parameter. At high temperatures, equilibrium can be reached quickly, but high-energy states are almost as likely as low-energy states. By gradually lowering the temperature during search, the system stays close to equilibrium while the probabilities of low-energy states continues to rise. In the zero temperature limit, only the most plausible models have positive probability. This technique is called "simulated annealing" because of the similarity to annealing in physical systems in order to reach low energy (crystalline) states. At high temperatures, energy differences between states are largely ignored and the probability of moving to a new state is always near one half. By changing state often, the system does a lot of searching, but by ignoring energy differences the search is not very discriminating. As the temperature is lowered, the system spends more of its time in relatively good states, because it has a lower probability of moving out of them. When the temperature becomes numerically much smaller than the minimum energy difference between adjacent states, the probability of ever occupying the higher-energy state becomes negligible (see equation 2.1). The system settles into a local energy minimum, from which all moves are uphill in energy, and for all practical purposes stops searching. Simulated annealing has been used to solve optimization problems by a number of researchers [Kirkpatrick *et al.*, 1983, Geman and Geman, 1984, Hinton and Sejnowski, 1986].

Calculating the state transition probabilities necessary for performing stochastic simulation is straightforward, even though the probability distribution itself is never computed explicitly. Using equation 2.1, the probability ratio between any two states is an exponential function of their energy difference. In order to make this calculation simple, the mapping between models and energy should be one where the differences between energies of pairs of accessible states is efficiently computable.

Geman and Geman [1984] prove that if all states are eventually accessible from each other, and if this procedure is carried out long enough, an equilibrium distribution will be reached, and that equilibrium distribution is the Boltzmann Distribution. An equilibrium distribution is one in which the probability of being in any state is independent of the starting state.

Boltzmann Machines [Hinton and Sejnowski, 1986] are a special case of this procedure in which the energy of a model is the sum of weighted pairwise products of unit states:

$$E_\alpha = -\frac{1}{2} \sum_{i \neq j \in units} w_{ij} s_i^\alpha s_j^\alpha$$

s_i^α is the state of unit i in global state α, where a state of one means true and zero means false. $w_{ij} = w_{ji}$ is the weight on the link between units i and j. If $w_{ij} > 0$, states in which both units are on have lower energy, so the constraint is excitatory; negative weights are inhibitory. Since every constraint involves exactly two units, Boltzmann Machines can be represented as graphs where the weights label the links. They are formally quite different from Bayesian belief networks, however.[3]

In Boltzmann Machines, the potential moves from any state are those states that differ from the current one in the value of a single unit. The difference in energy between two such states is called the unit's *energy gap,*

$$\Delta E_k = \sum_i w_{ki} s_i$$

A unit can determine its energy gap locally, by consulting the state of only neighboring units.

If there are many fairly good states, but traveling between them entails entering intermediate states with high energy, it is unlikely that the absolute best states will be found in reasonable time. Thus the topography of the energy space is important for good performance. If the domain is "nearly decomposable" [Simon, 1981] and the parameters

---

[3] Pearl [1987] discusses the relationship between Bayesian belief networks and Boltzmann Machines.

into which it naturally decomposes are represented by disjoint sets of units, the allowable moves will be "nearly independent" of one another. The energy space will be relatively smooth, and conducive to hill climbing.[4] The accessibility function acts as a divide and conquer heuristic. In contrast, if the states were all accessible from one another, there would be no local minima. However there would also be no concept of smoothness, and no benefit from well decomposed representations. The system would take random samples from the exponential search space.

3.5 μKLONE Energy Functions

It is impossible to represent the probability distribution specified by a μKLONE KB in terms of binary constraints over units representing atomic propositions. One version of μKLONE solved this problem by adding extra units to capture higher-order relations, and used the above form of the energy equations [Derthick, 1987]. μKLONE now uses a more general model in which the individual constraints are not restricted to be the pairwise product of unit states, but can be more general functions involving any number of unit states, including addition, multiplication, and exponentiation (see section 2.6). The energy difference between adjacent models can still be found in constant time for these functions.

The search algorithm described next, which is the one μKLONE actually uses, requires computing the derivative of the energy function in order to do hill climbing. Since min has discontinuous derivatives it is less than ideal for this search technique. Its derivative is zero for all arguments except the smallest, for which the derivative is one. If the two smallest arguments are close to one another, the derivative changes discontinuously for small changes in the state of each unit. It would be much better if the derivative could be divided among all the arguments, with the biggest share going to the lowest ones. Generalized mean values [Rivest, 1988] have the desired effect. One way to define the generalized mean value of a vector is

---

[4]Of course I mean Australian hill climbing, since the most plausible models have the *lowest* energy.

p	$M_p(a)$	$\frac{\partial M_p(a)}{\partial a_1} / \sum_i \frac{\partial M_p(a)}{\partial a_i}$
-1	.317	.52
-2	.287	.61
-4	.257	.74
-8	.233	.88
-16	.218	.98
-32	.209	.999

Figure 3.1: How the approximate min function behaves for the vector $a = (.20\,.25\,.40\,.90)$, as p approaches $-\infty$, and how much of the derivative is attributable to the smallest argument.

$$M_p(a) = \left(\frac{1}{n} \sum_{i=1}^{n} a_i^p \right)^{1/p} \tag{3.1}$$

For $p = 1$ this is just the ordinary arithmetic mean, and as $p \to \infty$ it becomes the max function. As $p \to -\infty$ it becomes the min function. Table 3.1 lists the value of the function for various p. Currently μKLONE uses $p = -16$. Some constraints also use the same function to approximate max instead of using AND constraints, in which case $p = +16$. For smaller values, the system would regard an OR constraint with one argument true, and the rest false, as partially unsatisfied. It would waste too much effort trying to satisfy more of the arguments. For larger values of p, the energy barriers between states with different arguments satisfied would be too large, and the system would commit itself too soon.

3.6 Units with Intermediate Truth Values

Stochastic simulation is a slow process. In order to ensure that the system can extricate itself from local minima, it sometimes makes moves that are uphill in energy. Usually these moves are counterproductive, and they result in lost search time. An alternative to getting out of local minima using a stochastic algorithm is smoothing the energy space so the search is unlikely to encounter local minima. Hopfield [1984] introduced a technique similar to annealing, which has been called "simulated ironing" because it smoothes out wrinkles in the energy space [Denker et al., 1987]. Hopfield and Tank networks use units with continuous states between zero and one, and a deterministic gradient descent search is often successful in finding good solutions. In cases where the search succeeds, it is typically an order of magnitude faster than Boltzmann Machines [Marroquin, 1985, Peterson and Anderson, 1987].

Well defined models correspond to the corners of a hypercube, where all unit states are zero or one. By enlarging the search space to include the interior of the hypercube, a more purposeful, efficient search is possible. The energy functions described above are expressed in terms of addition, subtraction, multiplication, division (by a positive constant), and exponentiation, and so they, as well as their derivatives, are well defined over the expanded space. By starting the search in the center of the space, where all states are $\frac{1}{2}$, gradient descent can be used. Since only corners correspond to models, interior local minima are potentially a problem. However, if all terms in the energy function are at most linear in the state of any given unit, no interior point will be a local minimum, so the search will always terminate at a corner.

Gradient descent tends to be faster because each step of the search is sensitive to changes in energy along every axis, rather than just one. To the extent that the energy space is smooth, there will be broad basins of attraction in the direction of the corners with the lowest energy. If the deepest basins are the broadest, then the basin for the best model will extend the farthest toward the center of the search space. This is the rationale for starting the search at the point where all states are $\frac{1}{2}$. In search spaces where there is a high degree of symmetry, there may be many equally good and similarly shaped basins of attraction, so a small random offset must be added to the initial states to break symmetry. μKLONE search spaces are highly irregular, however, so this has not been necessary.

The energy function as defined above is less than ideal for searching because the "continental divides" of the various basins of attraction encroach far into the center of the search space, forcing the system to make decisions early. In a Hopfield and Tank network, another term is added to the Boltzmann Machine energy equation to smooth the space further:[5]

---

[5]This description leaves out some parameters of the Hopfield and Tank model that will not be used in this thesis, and changes the notation to make it more like Boltzmann Machines.

$$E = E_{Boltzmann} + \sum_i \int_0^{s_i} g^{-1}(s)\,ds$$

where $g(u) = \frac{1}{1+e^{-u/T}}$, and so $g^{-1}(s) = T \cdot \log \frac{s}{1-s}$. T stands for temperature, which has the same meaning here as in the Boltzmann equation and the free energy equation.

At high temperatures the second term dominates, but it goes to zero as T does. It is minimized at $s_i = \frac{1}{2}$, so early in the search states of units which are relatively unimportant in determining the global energy take on values near $\frac{1}{2}$. As T is gradually lowered, the first units whose states take on extreme values are those representing the most important propositions. By deferring commitments on less important propositions, shallow local minima resulting from their interactions are avoided.

Hopfield and Tank introduce another modification, which is intended to make their model more closely resemble neurons. Each unit is modeled as an amplifier with finite input resistance and capacitance, and with transfer function g. The "energy calculation" is done on the input side of the amplifier, and the trajectory of the circuit is given by the dot product of the energy gradient with the vector of derivatives of the transfer function. The circuit still monotonically decreases the energy function, and for the purposes of this thesis, the difference from steepest descent is unimportant.

μKLONE's various implementations have alternated between using the Boltzmann search algorithm [Hinton and Sejnowski, 1983, Hinton and Sejnowski, 1986] and the Hopfield and Tank algorithm [Hopfield, 1984]. Before the specialized constraint types, which are described in section 3.7.1, were used to make the center of the hypercube relatively stable and smooth, the ability of Boltzmann Machines to escape local minima sometimes enabled it to solve problems that the Hopfield and Tank algorithm could not. However the noisiness of the Boltzmann search made tuning hard and solution times long. A hybrid model [Derthick and Tebelskis, 1988] in which units take on states intermediate between zero and one, yet are still stochastic, benefits from both the smoother energy space of the Hopfield and Tank model, and the ability to escape local minima of the Boltzmann model. For a time this hybrid algorithm's ability to mimic either strategy as well as a continuous range of intermediate ones suggested its superiority. When run fully deterministically, it is slightly inferior to the Hopfield and Tank model, however. If the

38

ability to escape local minima is required, it may still be the best approach. Yet using domain-specific non-linear constraints to eliminate some of the energy barriers that cause local minima in the first place has worked much better than any method of getting out again. For instance, early version of μKLONE used $\times$ to translate disjunction instead of min, and produced much worse search spaces.

The Hopfield and Tank model carries with it no guarantee of ever finding optimal solutions, however, and is one of the reasons the system as built does not fully obey μKLONE's formal theory of mundane reasoning. The Boltzmann Machine search algorithm does have such a guarantee [Geman and Geman, 1984], but the time bound is exponential and so the guarantee is not reassuring.

3.7 Modifications to Energy Function

3.7.1 New kinds of Constraints

Even using the Hopfield and Tank algorithm, the basic energy functions of section 2.6 do not always give good performance. As the search moves away from the center of the space, it enters basins of attraction containing ever fewer models. The algorithm is most successful if committing to basins containing only a few models can be delayed as long as possible. By making the constraints' contribution to the energy function as flat as possible near the center of the space, the system can explore much of the space before making commitments. For instance if a short chain of inference makes p seem likely, that unit will become more active early on. If a longer chain of inference, which takes longer to assert itself, later negates the argument for p, it is desirable for the state of p to decay back to $\frac{1}{2}$. If the space is relatively flat, the extra energy term that adds a concave upward component to the whole space will be able to pull p back toward its uncommitted state.

Using the basic energy functions, the energy surface defined by implications is not flat in the center of the space. When $p \to q$ is implemented as $\neg p \vee q$, the energy function is $\min((1 - p), q)$, whose derivative is, using the generalized mean value approximation, $-\frac{1}{2}$ with respect to p and $\frac{1}{2}$ with respect to q. So the system will drift toward models where

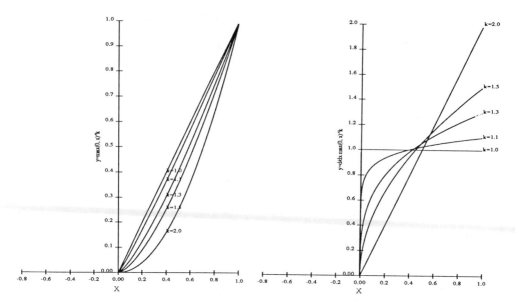

Figure 3.2: Energy and its derivative versus difference in state for IMPLIES constraints, for various exponents.

p is false, even though there are equally good models where p is true. The solution is to introduce a special IMPLIES constraint,[6] in which the energy contribution is a function of the difference in states: $E = [\max(0, p - q)]^k$ (see figure 3.2). It is also convenient to define (EQUIV a b) $\equiv$ (AND (IMPLIES a b) (IMPLIES b a)). With this formulation, the states will decay back to $\frac{1}{2}$ from anywhere in the space, in the absence of other constraints. The effect of k is discussed below.

This same energy function can be used to implement ATLEAST, ATMOST, or EXACTLY constraints as well:

$\left(\text{ATLEAST } n \ p_1 \ p_2 \cdots p_k\right) \equiv$

      (IMPLIES (AND (NOT p_1) (NOT p_2) $\cdots$ (NOT p_k)) (AND $\underbrace{\text{FALSE} \cdots \text{FALSE}}_{n \ times}$))

$\left(\text{ATMOST } n \ p_1 \ p_2 \cdots p_k\right) \equiv$

      (IMPLIES (AND $\underbrace{\text{FALSE} \cdots \text{FALSE}}_{n \ times}$) (AND (NOT p_1) (NOT p_2) $\cdots$ (NOT p_k)))

$\left(\text{EXACTLY } n \ p_1 \ p_2 \cdots p_k\right) \equiv$

---

[6] Interestingly, possibility theory also has a special rule for implication, rather than relying on the classical logic equivalence $a \to b \equiv \neg a \vee b$. The truth value for "if C_1 then C_2" is $1 \wedge (1 - \tau_1 + \tau_2)$, where the τ's are the truth values of the C's.

40

$$(\text{EQUIV } (\text{AND } (\text{NOT } p_1) (\text{NOT } p_2) \cdots (\text{NOT } p_k)) (\text{AND } \underbrace{\text{FALSE} \cdots \text{FALSE}}_{n \ times}))$$

where FALSE is constraint whose energy is always one.

There is another new constraint type, used to make the effect of a constraint felt more strongly in one direction than the other. Sometimes tentative evidence for proposition p should be taken as evidence for q, but tentative evidence against q should not affect belief in p. For instance if $(\text{ATLEAST } n - 1 \ a_1 \cdots a_n)$, the equilibrium state of unit a_1 is close to $\frac{1}{n}$. If a further constraint is added, $(\text{IMPLIES } a_1 \ p)$, the equilibrium state of p would be forced to a similar value. Here the search is moving away from the center of the search space, and possibly making an irrevocable choice that p, when there are no constraints that can only be satisfied if p. Therefore the energy of units like a_1 is raised to a high power, so unless the system is very certain it should be on, it will have negligible effect.[7] This is done with a VERY constraint, and the energy is $1 - (1 - E_{component})^k$. In words, $(\text{VERY } p)$ is false unless p is very nearly true. It is also convenient to define the dual, $(\text{PRETTY } p) \equiv (\text{constraintnot } (\text{VERY } (\text{NOT } p)))$, which is true unless p is very nearly false. Table A.2 summarizes all the constraints μKLONE uses.

3.7.2 More effective inference chaining

In logic, conclusions reached using long chains of inference are just as certain as the axioms themselves. In connectionist networks where truth values are replaced by activation strengths, it can be much more difficult to correctly propagate activation down long causal chains. The most obvious problems are attenuation and delay. If unit p is asserted to be on with unit strength, and the two implications $p \rightarrow q$ and $q \rightarrow r$ are also asserted with unit strength, the unit representing p will be on more than halfway, but less than fully on. Therefore q will have a smaller derivative than p, and its activation will be between one half and that of p's. The activation of each succeeding unit in the chain will decay exponentially to the resting activation, one half. Further, the time it takes for the states to rise from their initial values and begin to affect succeeding units introduces a delay that increases with the length of the chain.

---

[7]There is a similar operator in possibility theory, where "very p" is translated by squaring the truth value of p.

There are also problems when different assertions in the chain have different weights. For instance if the assertion p has unit weight, but the implications have weight 10, the energy derivative of unit r will be 10 times as large as it "ought" to be. "Ought" is in quotes because no theory has yet been given for what the energy derivatives ought to look like in the interior of the hypercube beyond the appeal for smoothness in the preceding section. A helpful physical analogy can be appealed to however. Section 2.6 presented an example of inheritance reasoning in which μKLONE was contrasted with NETL because of its "strongest path" heuristic for choosing among conflicting defaults. The strength of a path should be like the strength of a physical chain: the strength of its weakest link. In the path $p \to q \to r$, if another assertion introduces a positive energy derivative for the unit p, that same "force" for asserting p should be transmitted to units q and r. From its initial state of $\frac{1}{2}$, the state of unit p will become more true until the derivative of the implication $p \to q$ exactly cancels the derivative of the outside force. Under these conditions the derivative of the implication with respect to q's state should be such that it feels the same force toward true that p feels. Mathematically, the sum of the derivatives of the units in an implication constraint should be zero. For the original implementation of implications this condition was not met in general: the energy of the constraint (OR (NOT p) q) is $(1 - p) \times q$, and

$$\frac{\partial E}{\partial p} + \frac{\partial E}{\partial q} = -q + (1 - p)$$

For the special IMPLIES constraint the condition does hold:

$$E = \max(0,\ p - q)^k = f(p - q)$$
$$\frac{\partial E}{\partial p} + \frac{\partial E}{\partial q} = \frac{\partial f}{\partial (p-q)} \cdot \frac{\partial (p-q)}{\partial p} + \frac{\partial f}{\partial (p-q)} \cdot \frac{\partial (p-q)}{\partial q} = \frac{\partial f}{\partial (p-q)}(1 - 1) = 0$$

Correct propagation depends on an equilibrium, or static, situation. If the forces are not yet balanced, the unit states will be changing and the sum of the derivatives is not necessarily zero. In order to reach equilibrium in this example, p's state must become more true than q's to the point where the energy derivative of the implication constraint (figure 3.2b) equals the external derivative. For values of k closer to 1.0, the curve is steeper, and so p's state will have to change less. The effect of k can be thought of as the elasticity of the chains. Low k's therefore result in "tighter" responses. Since the

42

state of a unit is bounded, there is a limit to how much force an implication constraint can transmit, which is the certainty of the assertion times k. However up to that limit, the constraint will transmit exactly as much force as is applied to it. Thus the problem of non-uniform certainties has also been solved. A path really will be as strong as its weakest link.

In principle one would want k as close to 1.0 as possible so that forces can be transmitted while the unit states remain near $\frac{1}{2}$, and so the maximum force a constraint can transmit is not too much higher than its certainty. However the simulation proceeds in finite steps; each unit is probed and changes its state by a small constant times its derivative. As k gets smaller, the energy becomes ever more sensitive to small changes in state, so the constant has to shrink to prevent wild oscillations in the unit states. μKLONE uses $k = 1.5$ as a compromise.

The analogy also extends to branching chains. If p implies q and r and s, and there are forces trying to turn all three consequents off, the force on p should be the sum of the three forces. Mathematically, the sum of the forces should still equal zero. When this constraint is implemented as (IMPLIES p (AND q r s)) this relation is exactly true. When it is implemented using MAX instead of AND, the relation holds approximately.

3.8 Other Techniques

Finding a most plausible model is a task of optimizing a function defined over the corners of a hypercube. Connectionist models are one class that have been concerned with optimizing these kinds of functions. Another related class of models are genetic algorithms [Holland, 1986]. In fact SIGH [Ackley, 1987] combines characteristics of both types of models. It would be interesting to compare the performance of some of these other models to the Hopfield and Tank method. In addition, there are techniques that could be applied on top of Hopfield and Tank. For instance "momentum" [Rumelhart *et al.*, 1986a] often speeds up gradient descent in back-propagation connectionist networks by an order of magnitude.

These heuristic methods of finding plausible models either are not guaranteed to find optimal models, or the time required to find an optimal model is longer than exhaustive search would take. A better way to provably find optimal models is with an Assumption Based Truth Maintenance System [de Kleer, 1984, de Kleer, 1986]. These systems efficiently keep track of many models at once by clever indexing from propositions to the models in which they hold, and from (partial) models back to propositions. In μKLONE, for inconsistent theories there is no way to tell whether a particular model will turn out to be optimal without looking at all the alternatives, so the best technique is to be as efficient as possible in examining the entire model space. Still, any correct algorithm will take exponential time in the worst case.

4 Functional Description of μKLONE

μKLONE inherits its view of what a knowledge representation system should provide from its intellectual ancestors, the KL-ONE [Brachman and Schmolze, 1985] family of knowledge representation systems. The current generation, including LOOM [Mac Gregor and Bates, 1987], Krypton [Pigman, 1984], and Kandor [Patel-Schneider, 1984], provide a reasoning service to a higher level reasoning system. The KR component is intended to be a fast black box, and is not intended to be powerful enough to solve all the problems the reasoner as a whole is capable of. In a hybrid reasoner there may be many black boxes specialized for particular kinds of reasoning [Mac Gregor and Bates, 1987].

The KL-ONE family of KR systems uses a frame-style language for defining knowledge bases. The frame language is typically given a formal semantics in terms of a translation to first-order logic; however the frame-based syntax is important. It seems to reflect the way users think about domains, and it results in languages less powerful than full FOL, so more efficient reasoning algorithms can be used.

μKLONE differs from other KL-ONE-style systems in that there is a special purpose query language, which is quite limited in expressive power, and retrieves frames. The other systems typically include a general-purpose theorem-prover that attempts to determine the validity of arbitrary sentences.

45

4.1   Definition Language

4.1.1   Overview

The frame language (henceforth KB language) contains three ontological categories: concepts, roles, and individuals. Individuals are objects or actions in the domain. Concepts are classes of individuals, like PERSON. Roles are relationships between pairs of individuals, like HAS-MOTHER. If *has-mother(John, Sue)* then Sue is said to be a *role filler* of the HAS-MOTHER role for John. Concepts and roles are both *terms*.[1]

Ideally, terms are defined intensionally using a language the system itself can understand. This way the system can decide for itself what terms a new individual, or pair of individuals, instantiates. This process is called *realization* [Mark, 1981]. More abstract than realization is the process of *classification*, which involves relationships between terms, and is completely independent of anything in the world. One term is said to *subsume* another if an instance of the latter must be an instance of the former, no matter what the world turns out to be like. For instance, UNICORN subsumes RED-UNICORN even if in our world there are none. Being model-based, μKLONE must always have particular individuals in mind, and cannot find abstract subsumption relations between terms. Since users are presumably interested in facts about the world, purely terminological reasoning seems to have little functional importance. By caching subsumption relations, however, systems like Krypton are able to significantly speed up reasoning about the world.

Terminological reasoning sets KL-ONE-style KR systems apart from those in which concept definitions can include arbitrary Lisp code. These systems cannot understand the definitions, and therefore cannot use them in performing realization or classification [Brachman, 1985, Brachman, 1979, Woods, 1975]. Unfortunately, it is impossible for *all* definitions to be in terms a system can understand. There must be some base terms that

---

[1]In this thesis, term names are usually printed in SMALL CAPITALS, individual names are in the normal font and Capitalized, propositions are *italicized*, and pieces of μKLONE syntax are in `typewriter font`. Sometimes the normal font is used when the distinction between English and μKLONE is unimportant. To emphasize that "individual" is used in its technical sense to mean an element of the domain over which logical quantifiers range, rather than the ordinary sense in which it applies only to humans, I often use "it" to refer to individuals, even when they are known to be human. Appendix C summarizes all the typographical conventions used.

are unanalyzed. In μKLONE these terms are called *primitive*, and their extensions must be explicitly enumerated.

```
(DEFCONCEPT Person (PRIMITIVE))
```

introduces PERSON as a primitive concept.

Non-primitive concepts can be defined in terms of other concepts using DEFCONCEPT as well. However, the only use for non-primitive terms is as a notational convenience, similar to macros in programming languages. If a domain contains many facts about squares, it is more concise to avoid repeating "equilateral rectangle." There is a front end to μKLONE that immediately expands out all definitions, so that the actual reasoning system only sees assertions, and these refer only to primitive terms.

For instance in first fragment below, the two definitions do not generate any assertions. Expanding the third expression generates the base assertion which appears as the second fragment. Thus either of these input forms will assert that Bob has two properties: being male and having a filler of the HAS-CHILD role.

Fragment 1:

```
(DEFCONCEPT Parent (SOME Has-Child))
(DEFCONCEPT Father (And Parent Male))
(INSTANTIATE-CONCEPT Father Bob)
```

Fragment 2:

```
(INSTANTIATE-CONCEPT (AND (SOME Has-Child) Male) Bob)
```

4.1.2 Language Constructs

There are eight concept-forming constructs: DISJOINT, AND, OR, ALL, SOME (two types), FILLS, and RVM (see figure 4.1). Circular definitions are not allowed. A (DISJOINT c) clause means that the extension of the concept being defined is disjoint from that of c. For instance the definition of MAN may include (DISJOINT Woman). This makes WOMAN disjoint from MAN as well. WOMAN would have to be defined without reference to MAN to avoid circularity. (AND c_1 c_2 $\cdots$ c_n) defines a concept whose extension is

47

the intersection of the extensions of the c_i. Similarly, for OR clauses the result is the union of the extensions to the arguments. An (ALL r c) clause specifies that all fillers of the role r must be instances of the concept c. For instance someone's definition of SUCCESSFUL-PARENT might include (ALL Has-Child Professional). A (SOME r) clause specifies that there must be at least one filler of r. The definition of PARENT is (SOME Has-Child). With two arguments, as in (SOME Has-Child Male), there must be at least one filler of a given type. A (FILLS r i) clause specifies that an individual i fills the role r. For instance the definition of PROFESSIONAL-SAILOR includes (FILLS Has-Job Sailing). Role value maps (RVMs) specify set inclusion relations between fillers of different roles. For example

(DEFCONCEPT Deadbeat (RVM Has-Friend Has-Creditor))

means that a deadbeat is something all of whose friends are also its creditors. This is equivalent to

(DEFCONCEPT Deadbeat
  (DISJOINT (SOME (AND Has-Friend (DISJOINT Has-Creditor)))))

The meaning of nested constructs is always the same as if each nested construct is replaced by a new symbol whose definition is the form that has been replaced. For instance DEADBEAT could have been defined without nesting as follows:

(DEFROLE Not-Has-Creditor (DISJOINT Has-Creditor))
(DEFROLE Has-Non-Creditor-Friend (AND Has-Friend Not-Has-Creditor))
(DEFCONCEPT Non-Deadbeat (SOME Has-Non-Creditor-Friend))
(DEFCONCEPT Deadbeat (DISJOINT Non-Deadbeat))

There are five role-forming constructs: DISJOINT, AND, OR, DOMAIN, and RANGE. The first three have the same meaning as for concepts. A (DOMAIN c) clause specifies that the domain of the relation is subsumed by c.[2] A (RANGE c) clause specifies that the range of the relation is subsumed by c. For instance, the definition of HAS-EXPENSIVE-HOBBY

---

[2]In KL-ONE, specifying the domain of a role was done by "attaching" the role to a concept, and it was considered to affect the meaning of the concept. In μKLONE roles have equal status with concepts, and can be defined independently. Role definitions never have any effect on the meaning of concepts.

```
      <KB>   ::=   (<S>*)
       <S>   ::=   (DEFCONCEPT <concept> (PRIMITIVE))
              |    (DEFCONCEPT <concept> <concept form>)
              |    (ASSERT-CONCEPT
                       <certainty> <concept form> <concept form>)
              |    (DEFROLE <role> (PRIMITIVE))
              |    (DEFROLE <role> <role form>)
              |    (ASSERT-ROLE <certainty> <role form> <role form>)
              |    (INSTANTIATE-CONCEPT
                       <certainty> <concept form> <individual>)
              |    (INSTANTIATE-ROLE
                       <certainty> <individual> <role form> <individual>)
  <concept form>   ::=   <concept>
              |    (DISJOINT <concept form>)
              |    (AND <concept form>*)
              |    (OR <concept form>*)
              |    (ALL <role form> <concept form>)
              |    (SOME <role form>)
              |    (SOME <role form> <concept form>)
              |    (FILLS <role form> <individual>)
              |    (RVM <role form> <role form>)
    <role form>   ::=   <role>
              |    (DISJOINT <role form>)
              |    (AND <role form>*)
              |    (OR <role form>*)
              |    (DOMAIN <concept form>)
              |    (RANGE <concept form>)
     <concept>   ::=   <symbol>
        <role>   ::=   <symbol>
  <individual>   ::=   <symbol>
   <certainty>   ::=   <positive real number>
```

Figure 4.1: KB Language Syntax. OR, RVM and the two-argument SOME do not add to the expressive power of the language. They are macros that are expanded into the remaining constructs. Having both ALL and SOME is redundant, too, but both are implemented directly.

includes (RANGE Expensive-Activity). Role-forming constructs induce a taxonomy over roles; for instance R1 subsumes (AND R1 R2).

4.2   Assertion Language

In addition to their use for defining what is meant by various terms, these same constructs are used for making assertions about the world. In this respect μKLONE differs from other members of the KL-ONE family, where totally different languages are used for definitions and assertions. If an assertion is made about a term, it does not affect the recognition of instances of the term, but it does affect the beliefs about individuals, or pairs of individuals, that are recognized. For instance if it is *asserted* of SELF-MADE-MILLIONAIRE-PLAYBOYs that (SOME Has-Job), then it is not necessary to know that an individual has a job in order to conclude that it is a SELF-MADE-MILLIONAIRE-PLAYBOY, as it would be if this were part of the definition. However, anything that meets the definition of SELF-MADE-MILLIONAIRE-PLAYBOY will be believed to have a job.

There are two additional constructs that can only be used to make assertions, INSTANTIATE-CONCEPT and INSTANTIATE-ROLE. They assert that an individual instantiates a given concept, and that a pair of individuals instantiates a given role.

Assertions have certainties, which determine probabilities of the associated proposition as described in section 2.5. Formally, a certainty can be any positive real number. By convention, values in <0, 100] are used. Figure 4.1 gives the full KB language syntax, including both definitions and assertions.

The distinction between criteria for recognizing instances of a term, and facts necessarily true of instances of a term can be quite subtle. This is most acute in relation to primitive terms. Is a PERSON an ANIMAL by definition, or is this a necessary, but *a posteriori* truth? The domain specifications used in this thesis are open to debate; the important point is that either philosophical position can be expressed. In NIKL and Krypton, the difference in expressive power between definition language and assertion language tempts users to express sentences in whichever one it is expressible in, or in

50

whichever one leads to most efficient reasoning, rather than the one that carries the correct epistemological import [Haimowitz, 1988].

4.3   Relation to other KL-ONE-style Languages

μKLONE's KB language includes all the term-forming constructs of other KL-ONE-style systems except number restrictions, role chains, inverse roles, transitive closures, and structural descriptions. Number restrictions constrain the number of fillers of a particular role and come in two flavors, minimum and maximum. Role chains allow, for instance, the definition of a grandmother role as the composition of the mother role with the parent role. This makes it possible to assert that a role is transitive, although it is still not possible to define one role as the transitive closure of another. For instance, instances of (ROLE-CHAIN Has-Ancestor Has-Ancestor) can be asserted to be instances of HAS-ANCESTOR. Inverse roles allow the definition of HAS-PARENT by making it the inverse of HAS-CHILD. Structural descriptions provide for expressing complex relationships among the role fillers of an individual in terms of user-defined concepts. For instance if SUPPORT-RELATIONSHIP has been defined with two roles, HAS-SUPPORTER and HAS-SUPPORTEE, it can be used to define the concept ARCH. A structural description would force the HAS-UPRIGHTs of the arch to be in a SUPPORT-RELATIONSHIP to the HAS-LINTELs [Brachman, 1979].

In addition, LOOM has a simple mechanism to fill roles with default values [Mac Gregor and Bates, 1987]. This mechanism is much less powerful than default logic or μKLONE's certainties.

Within the KL-ONE family, there are a range of trade-offs that have been made between expressive power and tractability[3] (see figure 4.2). NIKL is the most powerful, containing the most constructs and using the standard semantics of first-order logic. Determining subsumption is undecidable [Patel-Schneider, 1988]. The designers are primarily concerned with typical-case performance, and have built a classifier that seems to find the subsumption relations that come up in practice, although it is incomplete.

---

[3]Patel-Schneider's thesis [1987, chapter 5] contains an excellent summary of the features and complexity of these languages, and is the source for most of the information in this section.

	NIKL	μKLONE	Kandor	$\mathcal{FL}$	$\mathcal{FL}^-$	Krypton
Concept-forming AND	•	•	•	•	•	•
Role-forming AND	•	•				
ALL	•	•	•	•	•	•
SOME	•	•	•	•	•	
General Number Restrictions	•				•	
RANGE	•	•		•		
DOMAIN	•	•				
DISJOINT		•				
OR		•				
FILLS		•	•			
Role Chains	•					•
Inverse Roles	•					
Structural Descriptions	•					
Subsumption Complexity	Undecidable	$\geq$NP $\leq 2^{2(n+1)^{nl \cdot 2^{n^3}}}$	co-NP	co-NP	P	P

Figure 4.2: Term-forming constructs of various KL-ONE-style KR systems.

It ignores DISJOINT statements completely, so DISJOINT is perhaps best considered part of the assertion language, and not as a term-forming construct at all. LOOM is a direct successor to NIKL and is more clear about exactly what subsumption relationships the classifier will find.

Much weaker than NIKL, but still intractable, is $\mathcal{FL}$, which contains only AND, ALL, SOME, and RANGE [Brachman and Levesque, 1984]. Brachman and Levesque show that eliminating RANGE results in a tractable language, $\mathcal{FL}^-$. $\mathcal{FL}$ and $\mathcal{FL}^-$ have never been implemented; they were put forward to illustrate how a small change in expressive power can have a drastic effect on the complexity of determining subsumption. Krypton [Brachman et al., 1985] is an implemented system with a correct polynomial-time classification algorithm.

μKLONE contains all of the constructs in $\mathcal{FL}$ and it can determine subsumption relations as determined by $\mathcal{FL}$'s semantics, so correct query answering must be intractable (see appendix B). To determine whether A subsumes B, the concept (DISJOINT A) must be defined. For a query that seeks to retrieve an individual that instantiates both B and (DISJOINT A), a zero energy solution exists if and only if A does not subsume B.

52

Patel-Schneider has investigated the complexity of a number of languages [Patel-Schneider, 1987] when they are given a semantics in terms of relevance logic, which is strictly weaker than first-order logic. He examines a language $\mathcal{U}$ that contains all the constructs mentioned above except DOMAIN. Even using relevance logic, $\mathcal{U}$ is still intractable. Removing number restrictions, RVMs, inverse roles, and structural descriptions results in a language that is tractable for KBs in conjunctive normal form, which is often a good approximation of real-world KBs. When OR and DISJOINT are also removed, the result is tractable for any KB using Patel-Schneider's semantics.

Patel-Schneider makes strong claims that his approach of weakening the language, so that sound and complete inference algorithms can be used, is the only appropriate way to do tractable knowledge representation. According to him, a system that cannot be given a model-theoretic semantics cannot be said to truly represent knowledge. He does not allow for the distinction made in μKLONE between competence and performance. Much of this thesis is concerned with developing a formal theory of reasoning, but always with the realization that it will only be an idealization of the system's actual performance. A formal declarative theory of the system's performance would be too complicated to be of any use.

If one accepts that KR systems are meant to represent objects in the real world, then Patel-Schneider's argument loses its force. Perhaps the term "apples" in his systems does represent something in a sense that μKLONE terms cannot. But it is certainly not the same thing represented by the English word "apples"—English can't be translated into the restricted formal logic Patel-Schneider advocates. Presuming that users really do want to represent apples, they will prefer the system whose behavior is most appropriate, regardless of whether that behavior can be deduced from a concise set of axioms.

4.4 Equivalent Logic Syntax

As already mentioned, the frame-based syntax is chosen to match the way users intuitively break up problems. Still it is useful to consider which theories, expressed in the usual logic syntax, have equivalents in μKLONE, because logic syntax is widely used and understood.

μKLONE's term-forming constructs are based on NIKL's [Vilain, 1985], which has a formal semantics [Schmolze, 1985] that uses a translation to first-order logic as an intermediate step. Although a full account of the meaning of a μKLONE KB requires consideration of the numerical certainties described in section 2.5, for consistent KBs the certainties can be taken to be one without affecting the set of most plausible models, and Schmolze's semantics applies. I will use lambda notation rather than the set notation he uses because it makes it easier to parse nested constructs, and I will only give two examples because the translation is just what you think it is.

(INSTANTIATE-ROLE 100 Ted Has-Job Sailing) means $has\text{-}job(Ted, Sailing)$.

(DEFCONCEPT Self-Made-Millionaire-Playboy

  (AND Person (SOME Has-Expensive-Hobby)))

means

$$self\text{-}made\text{-}millionaire\text{-}playboy \equiv \lambda x(person(x) \wedge \exists y(has\text{-}expensive\text{-}hobby(x, y)))$$

The KB language is weaker than full first-order logic primarily because of the limited way in which quantifiers can be nested. Only two constructs, SOME and ALL introduce quantifiers. Only SOME will be discussed because any KB can be expressed by replacing (ALL r c) with (DISJOINT (SOME r (DISJOINT c))).

The translation of (DEFCONCEPT a (SOME r)) is $a \equiv \lambda x(\exists y \ r(x, y))$. More quantifiers can be nested inside by incorporating either (RANGE c) or (DOMAIN c) in the definition of r, and incorporating another SOME in the definition of c. If DOMAIN is used, the expanded form of a's definition will be $a \equiv \lambda x(\exists y \ [r(x, y) \wedge c(x)])$, which is not a useful form of nesting. If RANGE is used, $a \equiv \lambda x(\exists y \ [r(x, y) \wedge c(y)])$, and the embedded concept will have access to a single usefully nested variable, the one just introduced with the existential quantifier. In general, further nesting results in $\lambda x(\exists y \ [r(x, y) \wedge (\exists z \ [r'(y, z) \wedge (\exists \cdots)])])$. Therefore in spite of the fact that the nesting can be arbitrarily deep, and that successive variables can be chained together with the role specification that serves as the argument to the SOME clause, the chaining is very rigid in that there is exactly one free

54

```
((ASSERT-ROLE 100 (AND)
   (DISJOINT
     (RANGE
       (FILLS
         (RANGE
           (SOME
             (DISJOINT
               (OR P
                 (RANGE
                   (SOME
                     (AND Q
                       (RANGE (SOME Q)))))))))))
   C)))))
```

Figure 4.3: Although any FOL proposition meeting the restrictions discussed in the text can be expressed in μKLONE, there is not always a perspicuous way to do it. This KB is equivalent to $\forall x \exists y \exists z \ p(c, x) \lor (q(x, y) \land q(y, z))$. It was produced by applying the constructive proof in appendix B, after un-nesting the predicates by hand. "(AND)" is the μKLONE way to say "TRUE."

variable in the scope of each quantifier—the one introduced by the immediately preceding quantifier. The role arguments are then fixed; the first one is always the free variable, and the second one is always the just-introduced variable. That is, the role arguments must be immediately successive variables, with no skipping, reversing order, or duplicate arguments. Thus neither transitivity, symmetry, nor reflexivity can be expressed.

More precisely, the equivalent language contains only one and two-place predicates, no equality predicate, and no function symbols (except constants). Every time a variable appears as the second argument of a predicate it must appear with the same first argument. If that first argument is a variable, it must be the immediately governing one. Any standard first-order formula meeting these requirements is contained in the language.

x *governs* y if the scope of the quantifier binding x properly includes that of the quantifier binding y [Dreben and Goldfarb, 1979]. x *immediately governs* y if there are no intermediate variables governed by x and governing y.

Syntactic restrictions on the arguments to predicates have been studied from a complexity point of view by Dreben and Goldfarb [1979]. Using these results, appendix B shows that query answering in μKLONE is decidable. Indeed it has the stronger property of *finite controllability*—for any definable KB a bound can be calculated, Ω, such that any satisfiable formula has a model smaller than the bound.[4] This property allows networks to be built that are guaranteed to find models, if any exist. Chapter 5 gives an algorithm for building provably correct networks using this (hyper-exponential) bound.

4.5   Query Language

After a knowledge base has been defined using the KB language, it is compiled into a connectionist network. Further interaction with the system takes place using a separate query language. Answering the queries involves a simulated annealing search, but the (patient) user need not be aware of the underlying connectionist implementation.

The query language is a pattern matching language for matching frames. The query itself is a partially instantiated frame, and the answer is a fully instantiated extension of the query that matches some individual in the system's internal model of its environment. For instance the query

```
((SUBJECT ?)
 (SUBJECT-TYPE Professional-Sailor)
 (WITH (ROLE Has-Hobby) (FILLERS Flying)))
```

tells the system to match some individual who is a professional sailor and whose hobby is flying. The answer would be in the same format, but the ? would be filled in with some particular individual.

Internally, the system extracts the instantiated parts of the frame to be matched, which are called the *presuppositions* of the query. In this case the presuppositions are that there exists some individual that is a professional sailor and whose hobby is flying. The presuppositions are combined with the permanent information in the KB, and a model is constructed that is the most likely interpretation of all this information. A subject is also selected to serve as the focus of attention within the model. The unspecified parts of the query are instantiated based on the part of the model within the focus of attention.

---

[4]The set of individuals a theory can refer to is called its Herbrand Universe. Although this set is generally infinite for μKLONE theories, finite controllability establishes that only a finite subset of these individuals have to be considered in seeking a model.

The reason an internal model is used, rather than matching directly on a representation of the KB, is that the KB may be incomplete and inconsistent. In order to retrieve coherent answers, some processing must be done to clean up and complete the KB. In traditional KL-ONE-style systems, this reasoning is accomplished syntactically using a theorem prover or a special purpose deduction system. In a model-based approach, construction of a model serves this purpose. It would be computationally cheaper to construct a model once and for all from the KB, and then do matching. But by finding a new model for every query, hypothetical or counterfactual presuppositions may be incorporated. In addition, by building the model starting from the subject of the query and working out toward indirectly-related knowledge, local consistency can be maintained around the focus of attention even when the KB as a whole is inconsistent.

A formal difference between the model-based approach and the syntactic approach is that the latter is given a sentence and answers whether it is valid or not. In finding a model, it is not necessary that a complete sentence be specified, and the answer is obtained by filling in missing information rather than verifying information. In addition, the system is satisfied when it finds one model consistent with the KB and presuppositions, while validity requires checking the sentence in all models consistent with the known information. Finding a subject, and making the subject match the query may involve assuming new facts and rejecting established ones. Of course, the system is biased to do as little of this as possible. Models violating a larger weighted number of asserted facts are always rejected, and among models violating the same number of assertions, those including more atomic propositions are always rejected. Excess atomic propositions represent unnecessary assumptions.

There are two constructs to specify the subject of a query, and four to restrict the role fillers. A query may contain a SUBJECT clause, which specifies the individual the query is about. It may contain an arbitrary number of SUBJECT-TYPE clauses, and the subject of the query must instantiate the argument of each of these clauses.

Constructs restricting the fillers of a role are grouped together, with one set of constructs for each role the query concerns. The query can have an arbitrary number of WITH clauses, each of which can have up to four subclauses relating to one role. The ROLE

```
<query>      ::=  ({(SUBJECT <i>)} (SUBJECT-TYPE <c>)* <with form>*)
<with form>  ::=  (WITH {(ROLE <r>)} {(VR <c>)}
                        {(FILLERS <i-list>)} {(MINIMUM-FILLERS <n>)})
<c>          ::=  <concept> | ?
<r>          ::=  <role> | ?
<i>          ::=  <individual> | ?
<n>          ::=  <whole number> | ?
<i-list>     ::=  <i> | (<individual>*)
```

Figure 4.4: Query Language Syntax. Query arguments and arguments to WITH forms may appear in any order. The number of SUBJECT-TYPE and WITH forms is limited by the implementation; four or five seems sufficient.

subclause specifies the role that the current WITH clause is about. A FILLERS subclause specifies particular individuals that must fill the role. A VR (value restriction) subclause specifies a type restriction that all role fillers must meet. A MINIMUM-FILLERS subclause specifies that there must be a minimum number of fillers of a role. The syntax of the query language is shown in figure 4.4. The syntax of answers is exactly the same, except without '?'s.

There are some limitations on the syntax imposed by the size of a particular network. A query is translated directly into a pattern of activity over a set of input/output units in the connectionist network. There must be a separate group of units for every clause that appears in the query. Rarely would more than half a dozen clauses appear in a query, so this architectural limitation does not seem to be important in practice. Second, a unary representation is used to represent the argument to MINIMUM-FILLERS subclauses. There is no need for arguments to MINIMUM-FILLERS to be larger than the number of individuals represented in the network. Even building this many units seems wasteful, because arguments to MINIMUM-FILLERS are usually very small integers. Therefore, the user must specify all possible integers that are allowed to appear as MINIMUM-FILLERS arguments at the time the network is built.

58

4.6   KB Language Semantics

Chapter 2 described the way certainties are used to determine the energies of models. The model best satisfying a query is one with minimal energy among those models satisfying the presuppositions of the query. The semantic interpretation of a KB must therefore retain enough information about the relative energies of models that when a query is applied, the set of most plausible models can be determined. If the semantic interpretation of a KB were simply the set of its most plausible models, it would be impossible to determine the appropriate new set given some presuppositions. To preserve the information about relative plausibilities, therefore, the meaning of a μKLONE KB is a function from models to energies. Together with the semantic interpretation of a query, this function determines the set of maximally plausible answers.

4.7   Query Language Semantics

A (model, subject) pair determines an answer to a query. The answer specifies the subject, together with a subset of the propositions that hold in the model: the concepts the subject instantiates, and a set of propositions about the role-fillers of some of the subject's roles. These role propositions include the fillers of the role, the maximally specific concept that the fillers instantiate, and the number of fillers. For instance in answering a query about Ted the professional sailor, the subject is Ted, and the model contains complete information about the domain, including propositions irrelevant to the query. The answer constructed from this pair will include only those propositions about Ted, for instance that he is a professional sailor, that all his children are male, or that he has at least one hobby. These propositions are meant to reflect the system's current beliefs, and are not necessarily logically consistent.

The meaning of a query is the set of (model, subject) pairs that could serve to determine an answer to the query. These are the pairs in which the energy of the model, given a KB augmented with the propositions in the answer that would be given, is minimal over all such pairs. For instance a model in which Ted's son is George may have the same energy as one in which his son is Bob, and both (model1, Ted) and (model2,

Ted) would be among the pairs from which an answer could be determined. Similarly, if a query does not specify a subject, different answers could be constructed from a single model by extracting the propositions about different subjects. The logical translation of the query constructs necessary for determining the logical form of the augmented KB is similar to the translation for the KB language. For instance, (SUBJECT-TYPE c) means $c(subject)$, and

    (WITH (ROLE r) (FILLERS (i_1 i_2 ... i_n)) (MINIMUM-FILLERS m) (VR c))
    means

$$\bigwedge_{j=1}^{n} r(subject, i_j) \;\wedge\; [\exists\, m \text{ distinct } k\text{'s}]\, r(subject, k) \;\wedge\; \forall x\, [r(subject, x) \rightarrow c(x)]$$

The unique name assumption is made over individuals. Although the meaning of a query, given a knowledge base, is fixed, picking an answer from the set of possible answers is non-deterministic. Equating the meaning of a query with a set of objects, any of which determine a single answer is similar to the "Set of Answers" semantics for questions [Harrah, 1984].

5   A Straightforward

Implementation

This chapter describes an inefficient system for finding optimal models of a knowledge base. The purpose is to push the formal approach as far as possible toward a connectionist architecture, in order to make the relationship of the actual system to conventional systems clearer. The model-based aspect of the reasoning is apparent, for the models over which the system searches are possible models in the model theory sense. In fact the system described in this chapter is provably correct for consistent KBs. The actual system, described in chapter 6, can be derived by a series of intuitively meaningful modifications to this architecture. The use of a query language is postponed until chapter 6.

5.1   Construction Algorithm

The idealized μKLONE search space is a direct representation of all models with no more than Ω individuals, where Ω is the bound calculated in appendix B on the number of individuals in the largest models that may have to be consulted. This section presents a general algorithm for constructing the search space and a set of constraints over the units such that a global network state represents a correct model of the KB iff the energy of the state is zero. All other states will have higher energy.

The Full Adder Problem introduced by Genesereth [1984] and analyzed in terms of counterfactuals by Ginsberg [1986] is used as an example domain. Figure 5.1 shows a schematic diagram of the circuit, and figure 5.2 illustrates how it is described in μKLONE. X, Y, and Z are binary addends, S is the one's bit of the sum, and C is the two's bit of the sum. The problem is to diagnose faulty circuit elements on the basis of the I/O behavior.

Before μKLONE can do diagnosis, the circuit description must be compiled into a connectionist network. The first step is expanding away all the defined terms, leaving

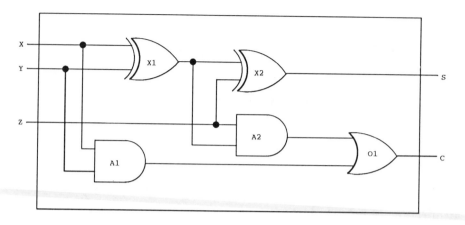

Figure 5.1: Schematic diagram of full adder

only assertions about primitive concepts and roles. If the size of the original KB is n, the expanded KB can be at most $O(c^n)$. For example, assertion (3) in figure 5.2 expressed in logic syntax is

$$\forall xy \; has\text{-}conn(x, y) \;\rightarrow\; \neg has\text{-}lower\text{-}val(x, y)$$

Upon expansion of the non-primitive role HAS-LOWER-VAL it becomes

$$\forall xy \; has\text{-}conn(x, y) \;\rightarrow\; \neg((node(x) \wedge \neg(node(x) \wedge has\text{-}val(x, High))) \wedge$$
$$(node(y) \wedge has\text{-}val(y, High)))$$

On the right hand side of the implication, the top line expresses (DOMAIN Low-Node), and the bottom line expresses (RANGE High-Node).

Next all quantifiers are expanded away, giving a propositional theory. The domain over which the quantifiers are expanded is the set of individuals explicitly mentioned in the KB as well as Ω made-up individuals, which are given arbitrary names. In the worst case, the size of the KB is further increased by a factor of order Ω^d, where d is the maximum quantifier nesting depth. d is bounded by n. The cumulative size is thus $O((c \cdot \Omega)^n)$.

The propositional theory is then put in a form where negation signs operate only over (ground) atomic formulas, and with no implication signs. The size of the KB is doubled

```
      (DEFCONCEPT Node (PRIMITIVE))
      (DEFCONCEPT High-Node (AND Node (FILLS Has-Val High)))
      (DEFCONCEPT Low-Node (AND Node (DISJOINT High-Node)))
      (DEFCONCEPT Gate (PRIMITIVE))
      (DEFCONCEPT Value (PRIMITIVE))

      (DEFCONCEPT And-Gate (AND Gate (PRIMITIVE)))
(1)   (ASSERT-CONCEPT 100 And-Gate
          (AND (DISJOINT Bad-And-1) (DISJOINT Bad-And-2)))
      (DEFCONCEPT Bad-And-1 (AND (SOME Has-Input-Node Low-Node)
          (SOME Has-Output-Node High-Node)))
(2)   (DEFCONCEPT Bad-And-2 (AND (ALL Has-Input-Node High-Node)
          (SOME Has-Output-Node Low-Node)))

      (DEFROLE Has-Conn (PRIMITIVE))      ;short for Has-Connection
      (ASSERT-ROLE 100 Has-Conn (AND (DOMAIN Node) (RANGE Node)))
      (ASSERT-ROLE 100 Has-Conn (DISJOINT Has-Higher-Val))
(3)   (ASSERT-ROLE 100 Has-Conn (DISJOINT Has-Lower-Val))
      (DEFROLE Has-Higher-Val (AND (DOMAIN High-Node) (RANGE Low-Node)))
      (DEFROLE Has-Lower-Val (AND (DOMAIN Low-Node) (RANGE High-Node)))
      (DEFROLE Has-Val (PRIMITIVE))
      (ASSERT-ROLE 100 Has-Val (AND (DOMAIN Node) (RANGE Value)))
      (DEFROLE Has-Node (PRIMITIVE))
      (ASSERT-ROLE 100 Has-Node (AND (DOMAIN Gate) (RANGE Node)))
      (DEFROLE Has-Input-Node (AND Has-Node (PRIMITIVE)))
      (DEFROLE Has-Output-Node (AND Has-Node (PRIMITIVE)))

      (INSTANTIATE-CONCEPT 100 Value High)
      (INSTANTIATE-CONCEPT 100 Node IN.2.X2)
      (INSTANTIATE-CONCEPT 100 Node OUT.1.A1)

(4)   (INSTANTIATE-CONCEPT 1 And-Gate A1)
(5)   (INSTANTIATE-ROLE 3 A1 Has-Input-Node IN.1.A1)
      (INSTANTIATE-ROLE 3 A1 Has-Input-Node IN.2.A1)
      (INSTANTIATE-ROLE 3 A1 Has-Output-Node OUT.1.A1)

(6)   (INSTANTIATE-ROLE 3 X Has-Conn IN.1.A1)
      (INSTANTIATE-ROLE 3 Y Has-Conn IN.2.A1)
      (INSTANTIATE-ROLE 3 OUT.1.A1 Has-Conn IN.2.01)
```

Figure 5.2: Excerpts from the μKLONE description of the full adder problem.

at most. Assertion (3) has by now become

$$\bigwedge_{x \in domain} \bigwedge_{y \in domain} \neg has\text{-}conn(x, y) \lor ((\neg node(x) \lor (node(x) \land has\text{-}val(x, High))) \lor$$
$$(\neg node(y) \lor \neg has\text{-}val(y, High)))$$

In the connectionist network, one unit is built for every atomic formula constructible from the primitive predicates over the above domain (see figure 5.3). The annealing search takes place in a space consisting of all assignments of truth values to the atoms. Given a propositional theory with restricted negation whose atoms map onto the units of a network, the mapping described in section 3.5 specifies constraints over the units that allow the network to find optimal models of the theory. Corresponding to each axiom is an identically structured constraint, where AND constraints stand for conjunctions, OR constraints stand for disjunctions, NOT constraints stand for negation, and ON constraints stand for positive literals.

5.2 Complexity

5.2.1 Space

The number of primitive concepts, C, and the number of primitive roles, R, are linear in the size of the KB. The number of individuals explicitly mentioned is also linear, but Ω, the number of made-up individuals is hyper-exponential in the size of the KB. I is the total number of individuals, both explicit and made up. Referring to figure 5.3, the number of Type units is $I \times C$, while the number of Role-Filler units is $I \times I \times R$. The total number of units is therefore $O(n \cdot \Omega^2)$.

Since the constraints built for the complete implementation are structured like the assertions, the total space to represent all the constraints is the same as the size of the expanded KB, or $O((c \cdot \Omega)^n)$. In contrast, the space complexity of the tractable implementation is only $O(n^3)$ (see section 6.3).

64

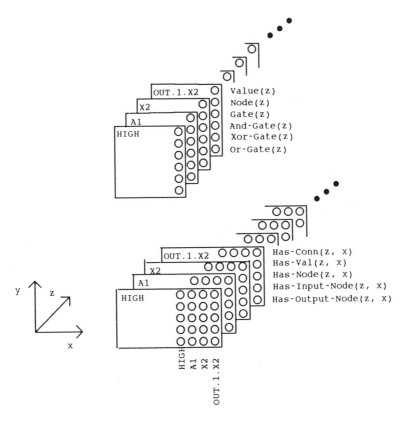

Figure 5.3: An object-oriented organization of the network built from the full adder KB. Each depth (z) plane contains two groups of units (rectangles), representing two kinds of knowledge about a single individual. The front plane, for instance, represents information about High. The column of units in the top rectangle of each plane represents type information, while the array at the bottom represents knowledge about relations to other individuals. Each row (y) of the array is concerned with one primitive relation, and each column (x) represents relations to a single individual. The units within complete boxes are exactly those required if the domain was shrunk to include only four individuals rather than $\Omega + 26$. In the full network both the number of planes and the width of the array in each plane would increase to this number.

5.2.2 Time

During the annealing process, as each unit is probed it must calculate the energy gap due to each of its constraints. To increase the efficiency of this operation, some state information is maintained by the constraints themselves.[1] In μKLONE constraints are implemented as Zetalisp flavors, and must handle four messages. The ENERGY-GAP message takes one argument, a specification of the unit whose energy-gap is desired, and returns the difference between the global energy when the unit is off and when it is on.[2] ENERGY takes no arguments and returns the global energy contribution of the constraint in the current state. INITIALIZE initializes the constraint. UPDATE-STATE takes two arguments, the unit whose state is changing and its new state. The state information maintained by ON, NOT, and AND constraints is just the energy. The state information maintained by OR constraints is the sum of the component constraint energies, each raised to the power p. This is just the summation in the energy equation (3.1) for OR constraints. With this information, it is possible to respond to the ENERGY-GAP and UPDATE-STATE messages in time proportional to the sum of the nesting depths of all occurrences of the unit in the component tree. For instance the time to calculate the energy gap of unit a given the constraint (AND a b (OR (NOT a) c)) is $O(1+3)$. Calculating ENERGY can be done in constant time. The time required for INITIALIZE is linear in the number of nodes in the tree of components.

At each time step of the simulation each unit is probed once, sending an ENERGY-GAP message to all the constraints that depend on it, and possibly an UPDATE-STATE message to the same constraints. During one time step, then, the time spent processing messages is the sum of the depths of all terminal nodes of all constraints. This is at least as great as the time required to initialize all constraints, which only has to be done once per query and so does not contribute to the overall complexity.

Therefore the time complexity to probe all the units once is the same as the total

---

[1] This makes networks using constraints less amenable to parallel implementation than standard Boltzmann Machines.

[2] This message is not used in the tractable implementation described in the next chapter, which uses the Hopfield and Tank search algorithm, rather than the Boltzmann Machine search algorithm. Instead of an ENERGY-GAP message, it uses dE-by-ds (derivative of the energy with respect to the state of unit), which takes the same argument, and has the same complexity.

space complexity of representing the constraints, $O((c\cdot\Omega)^n)$. In contrast, for the tractable architecture the time and space complexity are both $O(n^3)$ (see section 6.3).

5.3 Ginsberg's Query

As an example query, I will use the problem Ginsberg examines [Ginsberg, 1986]. His system is given a first-order logic description of the circuit and how its components work, assumptions such as that all connections function correctly, and boundary conditions at a particular time. The system then answers yes/no questions about the circuit. The interesting cases involve inconsistent boundary conditions, indicating a bug in the circuit. The counterfactual consequences of the boundary conditions include which circuit elements may be at fault.

At a certain time, exactly two of the inputs (X and Z in figure 5.1) are observed to be High, yet at the same time both outputs (S and C) are High. The correct behavior when two full adder inputs are high is that the carry is high, but the sum low. Following Genesereth's assumptions that the wiring of the circuit is correct, assuming the observations are correct, and making a minimal fault assumption, Ginsberg's system is able to prove, among other things, that one of the two XOR gates must be faulty.

In order for μKLONE to answer this query, there must be a mechanism for introducing constraints at query time, to reflect the particular observations. The next chapter describes this mechanism for the tractable architecture; here it is simply assumed that additional constraints can be calculated and integrated into the network at query time. In this example all that is required is the addition of five constraints, one for each of the observed node values. The ON constraints required are for the following units: $has\text{-}val(X, High)$, $has\text{-}val(Z, High)$, $has\text{-}val(S, High)$, and $has\text{-}val(C, High)$. A (NOT (ON x)) constraint is added for the unit $has\text{-}val(Y, High)$.

Which model is most plausible depends on the strengths of various constraint types. Least desirable is for the system to decide that AND gates do not have to work like AND gates, so the highest weights are assigned to assertions like (1) in figure 5.2, say 100. Next worst is to ignore the query's presuppositions, so a weight of 10 is assigned to the five constraints just mentioned. Among the particular facts about this circuit, it is more likely that a gate is broken than that connections have gone wrong. So a weight of 3 is assigned to statements like (5) and (6), and 1 to those like (4).

For various plausible answers, it is easy to add up the amount of constraint violation. In this case, there are many models that violate only a single constraint. For instance if the ON constraint $has\text{-}val(S, High)$ is violated, at a cost of 10, everything else can be made consistent, and similarly for the constraint on the input Y. Progressing inward, violating the assertion $has\text{-}conn(Y, IN.2.X1)$ or $has\text{-}conn(OUT.1.X2, S)$ allows an otherwise consistent model, at a cost of 3. Alternatively, the connections could be left alone, and instead the required value relationship between connected nodes could be violated. This would cost 100, though. Progressing further inward, violating the ON constraint $xor\text{-}gate(X2)$ costs only 1, and allows an otherwise consistent model. There are no other single gate failures that explain the behavior. Tracing back from the faulty output, S, suggests trying X1, but if its output were incorrect and everything else worked, the C output would be wrong.

The result of an annealing search is certain in this case, at least with respect to the crucial propositions. The boundary conditions will be satisfied, the values of the nodes will be correct given the inputs except for OUT.1.X2 and S, and $xor\text{-}gate(X2)$ will be false. However there are many units whose state is irrelevant to this problem, and whose final state is unpredictable. It may turn out that the made-up individual #:G0020 is an AND gate having #:G0011 as one of its input nodes. And #:G0011 may be believed connected to OUT.1.X1. Even worse, OUT.1.X1 may be connected to OUT.1.A2, as they meet the requirement for connectivity of having the same value.

The tendency to hallucinate freely can be eliminated by adding a small (NOT (ON x)) constraint to every unit in the network. This modifies the semantics so that the system finds the best minimal model of a situation. This invalidates the working hypothesis that true models are exactly those whose energy is zero. If the strength of the minimal model constraints is much lower than that of domain constraints, however, energies less than the weight of domain constraints can be considered zero for the purposes of determining the true models. The weight on these constraints should be less than the smallest domain-specified constraint divided by the number of units. Thus the system has two classes of constraints, *domain constraints* and *minimal-model constraints*.

5.4   Evaluation of the Architecture

Figure 5.3 spatially organizes the full adder network in three dimensions. Each z (depth) plane represents information about one individual, each y (horizontal) plane represents information about one predicate, and each x plane represents information about being related to one individual. The organization is strikingly uniform, and indeed it must be if the system is to consider any model involving the given domain and primitive predicates. But for real problems, and especially one like the full adder problem, it is inconceivable that any but a small fraction will ever be considered. Units like *has-conn(High, X2)* are essentially meaningless because High is not in the domain of HAS-CONN; a user would rarely be satisfied with any model including this proposition. This is a major disadvantage of compiling out all possible inferences into constraints over instantiated propositions. This finite state character is inherent in the connectionist approach [Pylyshyn, 1984]. In contrast, Ginsberg is free to add any propositions to his worlds as they are needed, but until then they are not taking up any space.

Another set of wasted units are all the ones relating to made-up individuals. Some theories may entail the existence of individuals not explicitly mentioned in the KB, so there is some need for extra units, but Ω will probably be ridiculously large compared to what is needed for mundane problems. And for the adder problem it is clear that no new gates, values, or nodes will have to be postulated to explain the behavior. In fact, there is complete information about what individuals belong in the circuit, and it would be cheating for the system to add any.

The full adder problem is both too easy and too hard for μKLONE. It is too easy because the domain knowledge is almost complete and unambiguous. This makes it well suited for Ginsberg's system, which is designed only to work with consistent KBs. The problem is too hard because conceptually sequential reasoning is required. There are clear causal chains from inputs to outputs. Although the chains are not very deep in a full adder, as a general circuit debugger μKLONE's ability to combine large amounts of conflicting evidence at once would be wasted, and its inefficiency at propagating information over long chains of constraints would be highlighted. In fact, such searches are inherently combinatorial, and I doubt the wisdom of using any general purpose system on such problems if domain-specific reasoners are available. In fact commercial circuit analyzers are quite domain-specific.

6   A Tractable Implementation

This chapter describes an alternative architecture in which searching for a model is faster, but the answer is no longer guaranteed to be optimal. Just as attempts have been made in syntactic systems to limit the form of the KB or the inferences that can be made in order to achieve tractability, in a semantic system the model space may be limited. It will be impractical to formally characterize the answers such a system will give, just as it is for syntactically limited KR systems. The usefulness of the approach can only be decided by empirical testing. A domain is presented in which good models are found for a number of queries, and the reasons this domain is suitable for the architecture are discussed.

6.1   Modifications to Straightforward Implementation

6.1.1   Caching Intermediate Results

Figures 6.1 and 6.2 show the tractable architecture used by μKLONE. It represents a single frame plus type information about all individuals, rather than a complete model. The Subject group represents the head of the frame, and the Subject-Type group represents the type. The Role-Fillers group represents the slots. The Role-Filler-Types group does not directly contribute to the representation of the frame, but background knowledge stored there constrains information explicitly in the frame.

The most important modification is the introduction of non-primitive predicates that eliminate the need for deeply nested constraints. In section 5.1, the exponential growth in the size of the KB resulted from the recursive expansion of definitions. Using definitions allows concise KBs because every construct that mentions the defined term shares an arbitrarily complex proposition. Since a direct representation of a model only makes

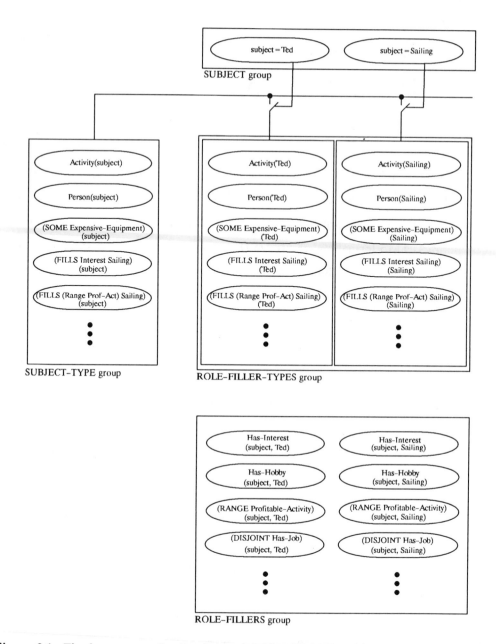

Figure 6.1: The four groups of units of the tractable μKLONE architecture. All that remains of the complete architecture of figure 5.3 is the type information about each individual, which is represented in the Role-Filler-Types Group. In this group, different individuals are placed in different columns, rather than at different depths as in the previous figure. Only a few example units in each group are shown. The Subject-Type and Role-Fillers groups represent complete information about a distinguished individual, the subject. These two groups together are analogous to one depth plane in figure 5.3. The Subject Group indicates which individual is the subject of the current query. None of the IO groups are shown.

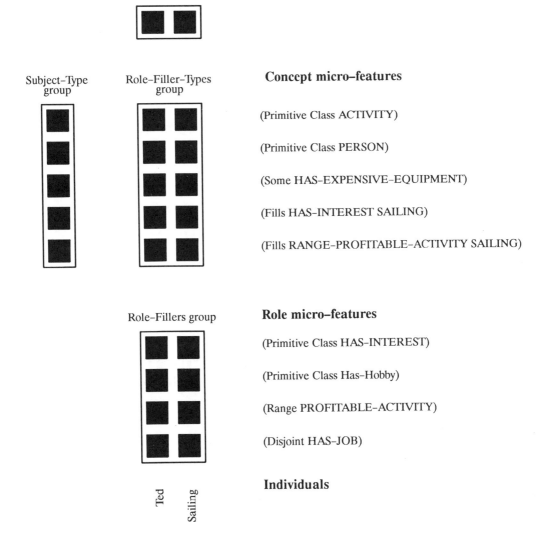

Figure 6.2: The same units as in figure 6.1, shown in the more space-efficient format that will be used in the remainder of the thesis. The individual unit names can be inferred from the labels on their row and column.

explicit the atomic propositions, the expansion is necessary in order to map the KB onto the straightforward architecture. By adding units to the architecture that represent complex propositions, the unexpanded KB can be mapped onto the architecture.

The disadvantage is that some units in the network will now represent non-atomic propositions like $(ALL$ has-job $armchair$-$activity)(Ted)$, whose states are definitionally dependent on that of other units. The complex predicates that form these propositions will be written in notation borrowed from the KB language. Thus (ALL Has-Job Armchair-Activity) is a one-place predicate whose extension includes individuals all of whose jobs are armchair activities. Units, and the propositions they represent, are written in italics (see appendix C).

The predicates from which the non-atomic propositions are formed include four types of one-place predicates: (DISJOINT c), (FILLS r i), (SOME r), and (ALL r c); and three types of two-place predicates: (DISJOINT r), (DOMAIN c), and (RANGE c). In the previous architecture, the representation was completely vivid [Levesque, 1986, Selman, 1987], with no possibility for meaningless representations. Now, with explicit derived information the search space contains self-contradictory states. These states are given a very high energy by defining new constraints, termed *structural constraints*, with weights much higher than either minimal-model or domain constraints. For example, there would be strong inhibition between the units $Person(Ted)$ and $(DISJOINT$ $Person)(Ted)$.

The computational efficiency gained by explicitly representing as unit states, accessible to many different constraints, what would be recomputed by each of these constraints in the vivid architecture outweighs this overhead. The number of units in the network is still $O(n \cdot \Omega^2)$, just as it was in the complete architecture. The constraint complexity, however, has been reduced from $O((c \cdot \Omega)^n)$ to $O(n^2\Omega^2)$.

Another disadvantage of not expanding the KB into its full clausal form is that the semantics are no longer fully respected. In particular, embedded conjunctions can contribute a maximum of one to the energy because no matter how many conjuncts are unsatisfied, the effect on the state of the unit that caches the value of the conjunction is the same.

74

6.1.2   Eliminating Most Made-Up Individuals

The second most important architectural modification is that the Ω made-up individuals have been reduced to only two. This does not reduce the power of the system very much in practice, since it reasons poorly about chains of related individuals in any case. It is expected that in reasoning about an individual, it may be necessary to consider related but unfamiliar individuals, for instance a mother, a job, or a favorite novel, but that mundane reasoning will rarely require simultaneous consideration of more than a handful of these made-up individuals. This reduces the number of units to $O(n^3)$ and the time and space complexity to $O(n^4)$.

6.1.3   Representing a Single Subject

The architecture described above may be practical as it stands. However by restricting the problems it can solve to those in which all relevant information is attached to a single individual, the complexity of simulating one time step of the annealing algorithm can be reduced from $O(n^4)$ to $O(n^3)$ and the unit complexity from $O(n^3)$ to $O(n^2)$. This factor of n comes from eliminating the information about each individual's role fillers. Instead, complete information is only represented about a single individual, the subject, which can map to a different individual for every query. With this restriction neither the full adder problem, nor any other problem requiring chaining through knowledge about multiple individuals, can be answered. If the KB is viewed as a semantic network, the system considers only individuals within a radius of one from the focus of attention, the subject, as well as their type information (see figure 6.3). For the full adder problem, complete connectivity information about the circuit would not be available, so the inconsistency of the boundary conditions could not be detected.

The limited knowledge still represented about all individuals is used to constrain the knowledge about the subject; the units standing for the identity of the subject in the Subject Group gate the type information about the individual who is the subject into the Subject-Type group (see figure 6.1). This is another source of redundant representations, and two more types of structural constraints are required to maintain a self-consistent

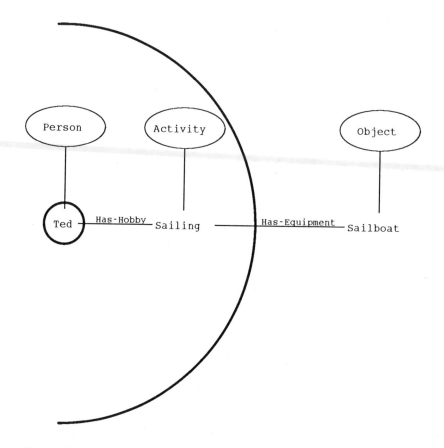

Figure 6.3: Illustration of the effect of representing a single subject on the knowledge accessible to the network. If Ted is the subject of the query, his type, his role-fillers, and the type of his role-fillers are accessible. The role-fillers of his role-fillers, such as Sailboat, are not available. The focus of attention is a circle of radius one, centered on Ted.

model. These constraints force exactly one Subject Group unit to be on, and force the subject's type to be the same as the type of the individual who is the subject.

In the complete architecture, enough information is explicitly represented to check constraints involving chains of role fillers. However in Boltzmann Machines, satisfying constraints over chains of units takes much longer as the chains lengthen (see section 3.7.2). Since the goal of μKLONE is to return guesses quickly, there would typically not be enough time to satisfy these constraints. Hence restricting the network so that the required information is not represented is more a recognition of an existing limitation than the introduction of a new one.

6.2   IO Implementation

All input and output concerns the subject, and is implemented by constructing groups of units that communicate with the central groups (those shown in figure 6.2). The user interacts with the system via the query language, so there must be an interface that translates Lisp symbols into patterns of activity over the IO units. This is done with a simple table that lists, for each individual, its position in the Subject Group; and for each concept or role, the pattern of bits corresponding to its defined properties. These patterns are then clamped into the appropriate IO groups, which are described below.

Specifying the subject is a trivial case. If the query specifies a subject, the pattern for that individual is clamped into the Subject group. In the case of all other query clauses, the information given may be incomplete, and so cannot simply be clamped into the existing network. For instance the *person* bit in the pattern for ANIMAL is off, meaning that animals are not necessarily persons. But if a query specifies (SUBJECT-TYPE Animal), it is incorrect to clamp off the *person* unit in the Subject-Type group, where the meaning would be that the subject is definitely not a person. So separate IO groups are built, named Subject-Type-IO-0, Subject-Type-IO-1, etc., in which a state of off means unknown rather than false. The inability to express falsity in the Subject-Type-IO-n groups is a reflection of the fact that queries may only require that the subject *does* instantiate a particular concept. The absence of a property can only be enforced using concepts whose definitions include `DISJOINT` clauses. A query can contain as many `SUBJECT-TYPE` clauses as there are Subject-Type-IO-n Groups, all of which must be satisfied by the subject.

Each `WITH` clause in a query may require up to four groups of units, to represent the `ROLE`, `FILLERS`, `VR`, and `MINIMUM-FILLERS` arguments. A small number of sets of four groups are built to allow several `WITH` clauses in a query. The groups are named Role-n, Fillers-n, VR-n, and MINIMUM-FILLERS-n, where n is instantiated to indicate which set the group is in. Each Fillers-n Group specifies particular individuals that must fill the role specified by the Role-n group; the MINIMUM-FILLERS-n Group specifies a minimum number of fillers; and the VR-n Group specifies a type restriction on all the fillers.

The constraints built from these IO groups to the central groups are called *presupposition constraints*, because their function is to add the presuppositions of the query to the domain knowledge contained in the KB. The strength of these constraints is generally somewhat higher than that of the strongest domain constraints. The strong domain constraints represent general beliefs about the world, which the agent is reluctant to change. On the other hand, the presuppositions of a counterfactual query should be taken more seriously than particular beliefs about the domain, or else the best interpretation of "If a, ... ?" would often be $\neg a$.

Finally, there are *complete answer constraints* to ensure that the answer returned in the IO groups is as informative as possible. Their strength is the weakest of any constraints, because the amount of information that can be returned should have no influence on the internal model that is built.

6.3   Complexity

This section goes into great detail about the μKLONE implementation, and can be skipped on first reading. The conclusion is that the space complexity of the network grows as the third power of the KB size, as does the time complexity of simulating a single time step in the annealing process.

6.3.1   Units

The number of units required is easy to calculate. The number of predicates must be linear in the size of the KB, because they must all be mentioned there. The number of individuals represented includes a linear number that are explicitly mentioned, and a constant number that are made up. The number of Role-Filler-Types units is the product of the number of individuals and the number of one-place predicates, while the number of Role-Fillers units is the number of individuals times the number of two-place predicates. The Subject group has a unit for every individual, and the Subject-Type group has a unit for every one-place predicate. There are a constant number of IO groups, all of which have $O(n)$ units. So the overall space complexity due to units is $O(n^2)$. The constraint complexity is discussed below.

6.3.2   Structural Constraints

The structural constraints ensure that the state of the network is self-consistent. Every place that knowledge is duplicated, whether in the same form or not, there is a requirement that all copies be equivalent. This is usually done with an EQUIV constraint.

For each constraint type, an example from the full adder problem is given. These examples are taken verbatim from the data structures given to the network building function, except that unit numbers have been replaced with more meaningful descriptions, and most of the constraints are shortened by using ellipses to indicate repetition of similar substructure with different arguments. For instance an OR may have as arguments all the units in one row of the Role-Fillers group, in which case only the first two would actually be listed. Rather than always choosing the first two units, I always begin with arguments that "make sense." For instance in checking to see if some individual is a NODE, I would choose the unit $node(OUT.1.X2)$ rather than $node(On)$. The ones that do not make sense still have to be included in the constraints that are built, but it is harder to understand the examples if they are listed explicitly.

79

Unique Subject

The structural constraint that there be a unique subject is implemented with two separate kinds of constraints. Between every pair of units in the Subject group is a constraint requiring either the first unit to be false or the second unit to be false. This ensures no more than one subject is represented. To ensure that at least one is, there is an OR constraint whose components are one ON constraint for every Subject unit. Recall that the time complexity for probing all the units once is proportional to the number of nodes in the tree of constraints. The complexity contribution of these two constraint types is therefore $O(n^2)$ and $O(n)$ respectively.

Example:

(WITH-WEIGHT *structural-wgt*

    (AND (OR (NOT *subject=On*) (NOT *subject=A1*))

        (OR (NOT *subject=On*) (NOT *subject=X2*))

        $\cdots$)

        (OR *subject=On subject=A1* $\cdots$)))

Consistent subject type

The structural constraint that the pattern in the Subject-Type group be the same as that in the column of the Role-Filler-Types group corresponding to the individual who is the subject is also $O(n^2)$. For every unit s in the Subject group, for every concept micro-feature f, an implication constraint is built, saying that if the subject is s, then the state of the Role-Filler-Types unit $f(s)$ is EQUIV to the state of the Subject-Type unit $f(subject)$. This implication is implemented using OR and NOT because IMPLIES constraints must compare states or their inverses: the special assumption it makes, that the constraint is satisfied if the energy of its arguments is equal, makes less sense if the arguments do not represent literals.

Example:

(WITH-WEIGHT *structural-wgt*

    (AND (OR (NOT *subject=A1*)   ;check all features of A1

80

```
                (EQUIV gate(A1) gate(subject)))
        (OR (NOT subject=A1)
                (EQUIV node(A1) node(subject)))

        ...

        (OR (NOT subject=X2)                        ;check all features of X2
                (EQUIV gate(X2) node(subject)))
        (OR (NOT subject=X2)
                (EQUIV node(X2) node(subject)))

        ...

        ...))                                        ;check all features of
                                                     ;the rest of the individuals
```

Defining non-primitive one-place predicates

The non-primitive one-place predicates are not independent of the rest of the model, so structural constraints are required to make sure the states of these predicates reflect their definitions. There are four categories depending on whether the predicate is a DISJOINT, ALL, FILLS, or SOME. The truth of the first of these can be determined just from the other one-place predicates that apply to the individual. Disjoint predicates can thus be enforced over all the columns in the Role-Filler-Types group. Determining the truth of the other predicate types requires knowledge of the individual's role fillers, and this knowledge is only available for the subject. Therefore these constraints are only enforced in the Subject-Type group. It is the lack of checking these other constraints that makes the tractable version of μKLONE incomplete.

- **Disjoint** Since extra one-place predicates are built for every clause that appears in the KB, any concept can be represented as a conjunction of features. A (DISJOINT c) predicate is true unless all the features of the concept c are present. The number of features involved is $O(n)$, there are $O(n)$ individuals whose type must be checked, and the number of disjoint predicates is $O(n)$, and for a total complexity $O(n^3)$.

81

Example:

(WITH-WEIGHT *structural-wgt*

    (EQUIV (NOT $(DISJOINT\ on\text{-}node)(OUT.1.X2)$)

        (MAX $node(OUT.1.X2)$ $(FILLS\ has\text{-}val\ On)(OUT.1.X2)$))))

- **All** These constraints must check the type of every filler of a role. In the example below, the outermost MAX does this, ranging over all individuals. For an individual, the constraint is satisfied unless both (the individual does not possess all the required concept features) and (the relation between the subject and the individual does possess all the required role features). Each constraint mentions $O(n^2)$ units, and $O(n)$ of them are required.

Example:

(WITH-WEIGHT *structural-wgt*

    (EQUIV $(ALL\ has\text{-}input\text{-}node\ off\text{-}node)(subject)$

        (MAX (NOT (MAX (NOT (MAX $node(OUT.1.X2)$

                                 $(FILLS\ has\text{-}val\ On)(OUT.1.X2)$))

                    $has\text{-}input\text{-}node(subject, OUT.1.X2)$))

           (NOT (MAX (NOT (MAX $node(A1)$ $(FILLS\ has\text{-}val\ On)(A1)$))

                   $has\text{-}input\text{-}node(subject, A1)$))

        $\cdots$)))

- **Fills** If a (FILLS r i) unit is on, then the pattern for the individual i filling the role r must be present in the Role-Fillers group. The pattern is of size $O(n)$ and there are $O(n)$ FILLS predicates, for a total complexity of $O(n^2)$.

Example:

(WITH-WEIGHT *structural-wgt*

    (EQUIV $(FILLS\ has\text{-}val\ On)(subject)$

        (MAX $has\text{-}val(subject, On)$))))

- **Some** A SOME predicate is satisfied if and only if some individual fills the specified role. This involves checking $O(n^2)$ Role-Fillers units for each SOME predicate, so the complexity is $O(n^3)$.

Example:

(WITH-WEIGHT *structural-wgt*
    (EQUIV $(SOME\ (AND\ has\text{-}output\text{-}node\ (RANGE\ off\text{-}node)))(subject)$
        (OR (MAX $has\text{-}output\text{-}node(subject, OUT.1.X2)$
            $(RANGE\ off\text{-}node)(subject, OUT.1.X2))$
         (MAX $has\text{-}output\text{-}node(subject, X2)$
            $(RANGE\ off\text{-}node)(subject, X2))$
        $\cdots)))$

Defining non-primitive two-place predicates

There are three kinds of structural constraint that correspond to the non-primitive two-place predicates resulting from DOMAIN, RANGE, and DISJOINT clauses in role assertions. For each predicate, separate constraints are built in each column of the Role-Fillers group. The DISJOINT constraints have the same form as the one-place DISJOINT constraints. There are $O(n)$ role fillers, $O(n)$ DOMAIN clauses, and $O(n)$ features to be checked, for a complexity of $O(n^3)$.

Example:

(WITH-WEIGHT *structural-wgt*
    (EQUIV (NOT $(DISJOINT\ has\text{-}higher\text{-}val)(subject, OUT.1.X2))$
        (MAX $(DOMAIN\ on\text{-}node)(subject, OUT.1.X2)$
          $(RANGE\ off\text{-}node)(subject, OUT.1.X2))))$

DOMAIN predicates require that the subject's type match the argument to the DOMAIN clause.

Example:

(WITH-WEIGHT *structural-wgt*

$$(\text{EQUIV } (DOMAIN\ off\text{-}node)(subject, OUT.1.X2)$$

$$(\text{MAX } node(subject)\ (DISJOINT\ on\text{-}node)(subject))))$$

RANGE predicates require that the filler's type match the argument to the RANGE clause. Example:

$$(\text{WITH-WEIGHT *structural-wgt*}$$

$$(\text{EQUIV } (RANGE\ value)(subject, On)$$

$$(\text{MAX } value(On))))$$

6.3.3   Domain Constraints

These constraints result from assertions about the domain, and are unidirectional implications. There are four kinds of domain constraints, corresponding to the four assertion forms in the KB language: ASSERT-CONCEPT, ASSERT-ROLE, INSTANTIATE-CONCEPT, and INSTANTIATE-ROLE. The last two are the simplest. If an individual is asserted to instantiate a concept, then an ON constraint is imposed on every feature the concept entails in the individual's column in the Role-Filler-Types group.

Example:

(WITH-WEIGHT <assertion-strength> $and\text{-}gate(A1)$))

Role instantiations can only be enforced for the subject. Each Subject group unit is connected with an IMPLIES constraint to every unit in the Role-Fillers group representing the conjunction of an atomic role and an individual known to be so related. The total complexity of each of these constraint types is $O(n^2)$.

Example:

(WITH-WEIGHT <assertion-strength>

(IMPLIES $subject=A1\ has\text{-}input\text{-}node(subject, IN.1.A1)$)))

The other two types are analogous, but the antecedents are patterns. For each ASSERT-CONCEPT clause, for each individual, an IMPLIES constraint is built in that individual's column in the Role-Filler-Types group. The antecedent units are the features of the first argument to the assertion, and the consequent units are the features of the

84

second argument. As an optimization, units that would be both antecedents and conse-quents are dropped from the consequent list. According to the formal theory, the energy penalty should increase linearly with the number of consequent propositions falsified, as would be the case if an AND constraint were used. However only MAX constraints can be arguments to IMPLIES constraints, which give much better dynamic behavior. Using MAX constraints, the energy penalty for the first violation is large, but that for succeeding violations approaches zero. This may actually be a feature: If an individual is asserted to be a bird, once it is established that it cannot fly, and has no wings, the certainty that it lays eggs would naturally decrease.

Example:

(WITH-WEIGHT <assertion-strength>

    (IMPLIES (MAX $and\text{-}gate\text{-}ness(A1)$ $gate(A1)$)

        (MAX $(DISJOINT\ bad\text{-}and\text{-}1)(A1)$ $(DISJOINT\ bad\text{-}and\text{-}2)(A1))))$

Here, AND-GATE-NESS is the name the system makes up to describe the primitive pred-icate that differentiates AND gates from other gates (see the definition of AND-GATE in figure 5.2).

Similarly, for each ASSERT-ROLE clause, for each individual, an IMPLIES constraint is built in the individual's column in the Role-Fillers group. Again the antecedent units are determined by the first argument to the assertion, and the rest determine the consequents. Both types of constraints have a total complexity of $O(n^3)$.

Example:

(WITH-WEIGHT <assertion-strength>

    (IMPLIES (MAX $has\text{-}val(subject, On)$)

        (MAX $(DOMAIN\ node)(subject, On)$ $(RANGE\ value)(subject, On))))$

6.3.4 Minimal Model Constraints

These constraints are used to make sure the model chosen is minimal over the set of models that best meet the domain constraints. All units in the Role-Filler-Types and Role-Fillers groups that represent *primitive* predicates are given a weak (NOT (ON x))

constraint. The values of non-primitive predicates are determined by the values of primitive predicates, and are not distinct assumptions. However the primitive predicates on which SOME, ALL, and FILLS predicates depend are determined by each individual's role fillers, and these are not represented in the tractable implementation. Hence it is not possible to determine exactly how many assumptions would be required to fill out a complete model. Still, it is a reasonable heuristic to treat SOME, ALL, and FILLS predicates as if they were primitive for the purposes of counting assumptions, and so they are also given a weak constraint to turn off in the Role-Filler-Types Group.

This approximation makes the energy of a model sensitive to which individual is the subject. That is, even if the implicit complete model remains the same, some views of it will be preferred because the subject has fewer role-fillers. Ideally, an extra penalty would be added proportional to the number of primitive role propositions true of all individuals other than the subject. While this number cannot be determined exactly, the number explicitly mentioned in INSTANTIATE-ROLE clauses is used as an estimate. Each Subject Group unit is given a (NOT (ON x)) constraint whose strength is proportional to this estimate.

6.3.5 Presupposition Constraints

Since the SUBJECT of a query is clamped directly into the central Subject Group rather than into a separate IO group, no constraints are required. Other presupposition constraints involve units in IO groups, none of which are shown in figure 6.2. Instead refer to figure 6.7, which shows the network built for the Ted Turner domain. For SUBJECT-TYPE clauses, the pattern in the Subject-Type Group must be at least as specific as that in each Subject-Type-IO Group. This requires an implication from every Subject-Type-IO unit to the corresponding Subject-Type unit. Subject-Type-IO units should have no effect on Subject-Type units unless they are being used for input, and are clamped. Using a VERY constraint makes it suitably asymmetric.

Example:

(WITH-WEIGHT *presupposition-wgt*

   (IMPLIES (VERY $gate(subject\text{-}IO)$) $gate(subject)$)))

There are three kinds of constraints that implement the FILLERS, MINIMUM-FILLERS, and VR components of WITH clauses. The FILLERS clause specifies that each individual represented in the Fillers-n group fills the role represented in the Role-n group. A presupposition constraint is built such that at least the cross product of these groups is on in the Role-Fillers group. Specifically, there is one IMPLIES constraint for every Role-Fillers unit, where that unit, in row r and column c, is the consequent, and the antecedents are the rth unit in the Fillers-n group and the cth unit in the Fillers-n group. Again, VERY constraints ensure that IO units only affect the central units if they are clamped.

Example:

```
(WITH-WEIGHT *presupposition-wgt*
    (IMPLIES (VERY (MAX <role-n unit> <fillers-n unit>))
        <role-fillers unit>))
```

The MINIMUM-FILLERS clause requires the subject to have a minimum number of fillers of the role specified in the Role-n group. The possible arguments for MINIMUM-FILLERS clauses must be specified at the time the network is built. Each MINIMUM-FILLERS-n group contains a unit for each possible argument. The query processor maps MINIMUM-FILLERS arguments onto patterns where units representing numbers less than or equal to the argument are on, and others off. The effect of MINIMUM-FILLERS clauses is achieved by counting the number of fillers on in the Fillers-n group. In a WITH clause that specifies arguments both for FILLERS and MINIMUM-FILLERS, the units in the Fillers-n group representing individuals declared to be fillers are clamped on, but the other units are not clamped. Otherwise other individuals that turn out to fill the role could not be counted towards fulfilling the MINIMUM-FILLERS requirement.

The MINIMUM-FILLERS-n group is connected only to the corresponding Fillers-n group. Each unit in the former group participates in one constraint. For the unit representing an argument of N, and where k is the size of the Fillers-n, the constraint is:

```
(WITH-WEIGHT *presupposition-wgt*
    (IMPLIES (VERY minimum-fillers-unit)
```

$$(\text{ATLEAST } N \; fillers - unit_1, \; fillers - unit_2, \; \cdots)))$$

The VR clause requires all the subject's fillers of the role specified in the Role-n group to instantiate the concept represented in the VR-n group. Every individual is considered separately. Given an individual, the constraints involve the individual's column in both the Role-Fillers and Role-Filler-Types groups, as well as the VR-n and Role-n groups. To determine if the individual fills the role, corresponding units in the Role-n group and the Role-Fillers column are compared. If for any pair, the former unit is on and the latter off, then individual does not fill the role, and does not violate the VR. If the individual does fill the role, then a pairwise comparison must be made between units in the VR-n group and the Role-Filler-Types column. If for any pair of units, the former is on and the latter off, the VR has been violated.

General Form:

```
(WITH-WEIGHT *presupposition-wgt*
    (OR (NOT (MAX (IMPLIES (VERY <role-n unit>) <role-fillers unit>)
                  (IMPLIES (VERY <role-n unit>) <role-fillers unit>)
              ···))              ;repeat for
                                 ;(role-n unit, role-fillers unit)
                                 ;pairs for each
                                 ;role micro-feature
        (MAX (IMPLIES (VERY <vr-n unit>) <role-filler-types unit>)
             (IMPLIES (VERY <vr-n unit>) <role-filler-types unit>)
         ···)))              ;repeat for each
                             ;concept micro-feature
```

6.3.6 Complete Answer Constraints

IO units in MINIMUM-FILLERS-n, Fillers-n, and VR-n groups always imply something about the fillers of the role represented in the corresponding Role-n group. That is, if they are asserted, some condition must be met by the units in the central groups. These units can always be turned off without violating any presupposition constraints. When

88

IO groups are being used for output, it is desirable that they return an answer that is as specific as possible. Thus these units are given a small ON constraint so they will come on whenever the condition on the central groups is met.

6.4   The Role Shift Problem

The Ted Turner domain is well suited for reasoning by satisfying multiple soft constraints. Unlike in the full adder problem, the KB is incomplete not only with respect to beliefs about individuals, but also with respect to what individuals there are. The set of beliefs about single individuals is complex enough that interesting reasoning can be done within μKLONE's architectural limitation of representing only a single frame at a time.

6.4.1   Informal Description

Imagine walking along a pier and meeting Ted, who is dressed as a sailor. Ted launches into an excited monolog on the influence of independent television stations on TV programming. It seems reasonable to conclude that Ted is a professional sailor, and that he is interested in television. If later it is discovered that Ted is a self-made millionaire playboy, the previous conclusions about Ted would probably be changed. While self-made millionaire playboys generally have jobs, they are unlikely to be involved in manual labor. Millionaire playboys often have ostentatious pastimes, so perhaps sailing is Ted's hobby rather than his job. Given that he has some job, the fact that he is interested in television suggests that that field may be his profession.

The domain description of figure 6.4 is an attempt to encode the original beliefs about Ted. The primary query considered in this thesis asks counterfactually, "If Ted were a self-made millionaire playboy, what would his job and hobby be?" The exact query is

```
((SUBJECT Ted)
 (SUBJECT-TYPE Self-Made-Millionaire-Playboy)
 (WITH (ROLE Has-Hobby) (FILLERS ?))
 (WITH (ROLE Has-Job) (FILLERS ?)))
```

89

```
(DEFCONCEPT Animal (PRIMITIVE))
(DEFCONCEPT Person (PRIMITIVE))
(ASSERT-CONCEPT 100 Person Animal)
(DEFCONCEPT Self-Made-Millionaire-Playboy
  (AND Person
       (SOME Has-Expensive-Hobby)
       (ALL Has-Job Armchair-Activity)))
(ASSERT-CONCEPT 100 Self-Made-Millionaire-Playboy (SOME Has-Job))
(DEFCONCEPT Professional-Sailor
  (AND Person
       (FILLS Has-Interest Sailing)
       (FILLS (RANGE Profitable-Activity) Sailing)))
(DEFCONCEPT TV-Buff (SOME Has-Interest Television-Related-Activity))
(ASSERT-CONCEPT 100 TV-Buff Person)
(DEFCONCEPT Activity (PRIMITIVE))
(ASSERT-CONCEPT 100 Activity
  (AND (DISJOINT Inanimate-Object)
       (DISJOINT Animal)))
(DEFCONCEPT Expensive-Activity
  (AND Activity
       (SOME Has-Expensive-Equipment)))
(DEFCONCEPT Armchair-Activity (PRIMITIVE))
(ASSERT-CONCEPT 100 Armchair-Activity Activity)
(DEFCONCEPT Vigorous-Activity
  (AND Activity
       (DISJOINT Armchair-Activity)))
(DEFCONCEPT Profitable-Activity (PRIMITIVE))
(ASSERT-CONCEPT 100 Profitable-Activity Activity)
(DEFCONCEPT UnProfitable-Activity
  (AND Activity
       (DISJOINT Profitable-Activity)))
(DEFCONCEPT Television-Related-Activity (PRIMITIVE))
(ASSERT-CONCEPT 100 Television-Related-Activity Activity)
(DEFCONCEPT Inanimate-Object (PRIMITIVE))
(ASSERT-CONCEPT 100 Inanimate-Object (DISJOINT Animal))
(DEFCONCEPT Expensive-Item (PRIMITIVE))
(ASSERT-CONCEPT 100 Expensive-Item Inanimate-Object)
```

Figure 6.4: Ted Turner domain definition, part 1.

```
(DEFROLE Has-Interest (PRIMITIVE))
(ASSERT-ROLE 100 Has-Interest (AND (DOMAIN Animal) (RANGE Activity)))
(DEFROLE Has-Job (AND Has-Interest (RANGE Profitable-Activity)))
(DEFROLE Has-Hobby (PRIMITIVE))
(ASSERT-ROLE 100 Has-Hobby (AND Has-Interest (DISJOINT Has-Job)))
(DEFROLE Has-Expensive-Hobby (AND Has-Hobby (RANGE Expensive-Activity)))
(DEFROLE Has-Equipment (PRIMITIVE))
(ASSERT-ROLE 100 Has-Equipment (AND (DOMAIN Activity)
  (RANGE Inanimate-Object)))
(DEFROLE Has-Expensive-Equipment
  (AND Has-Equipment (RANGE Expensive-Item)))

(INSTANTIATE-CONCEPT 50 Vigorous-Activity Sailing)
(INSTANTIATE-CONCEPT 50 Expensive-Activity Sailing)
(INSTANTIATE-CONCEPT 50 Expensive-Activity Flying)
(INSTANTIATE-CONCEPT 50 (AND Profitable-Activity Armchair-Activity)
  Corporate-Raiding)
(INSTANTIATE-CONCEPT 50
  (AND Television-Related-Activity
       Armchair-Activity
       UnProfitable-Activity)
  TV-Watching)
(INSTANTIATE-CONCEPT 50
  (AND Television-Related-Activity Vigorous-Activity Profitable-Activity)
  TV-Acting)
(INSTANTIATE-CONCEPT 50
  (AND Television-Related-Activity Armchair-Activity Profitable-Activity)
  TV-Network-Management)
(INSTANTIATE-CONCEPT 50 (AND  Professional-Sailor TV-Buff) Ted)
```

Figure 6.4: Ted Turner domain definition, part 2

The important KB definitions are: A PROFESSIONAL-SAILOR is a PERSON among whose HAS-JOBs is Sailing. A SELF-MADE-MILLIONAIRE-PLAYBOY is a PERSON with some HAS-HOBBY that is an EXPENSIVE-ACTIVITY, all of whose HAS-JOBs must be ARMCHAIR-ACTIVITYs. A TV-BUFF is something with some HAS-INTEREST that is a TELEVISION-RELATED-ACTIVITY. The critical assertion is that SELF-MADE-MILLIONAIRE-PLAYBOYs must have at least one HAS-JOB. Both HAS-JOBs and HAS-HOBBYs are HAS-INTERESTs.

When the μKLONE network constructed from the knowledge base is asked "If Ted were a self-made millionaire playboy, what would his job and hobby be?" the system must try to reconcile being a millionaire playboy with its previous knowledge about Ted, that he is a professional sailor and is interested in TV. The counterfactual premise conflicts with the knowledge base because sailing is a vigorous activity, and the jobs of millionaire playboys must be armchair activities. The initial impact of this conflict on the selection of a model is that sailing is likely to still be one of Ted's interests, but perhaps not his job. Since millionaire playboys must have expensive hobbies and only two activities known to require expensive equipment are in the KB, flying and sailing are the most likely candidates. Sailing is chosen because it is already thought to be an interest. The plausible substitution that sailing is Ted's hobby rather than his job is made because HAS-JOB and HAS-HOBBY are both subsumed by HAS-INTEREST, making it relatively easy to slip between them.

A millionaire playboy must have a job that is an armchair activity and a profitable activity. Both TV-network-management and corporate-raiding fit this category, but the former is chosen because it is known that Ted is interested in television. TV-acting is rejected because it is not an armchair-activity, and TV-watching is rejected because it is not a profitable-activity.

If the knowledge base did not specify that millionaire playboys had expensive hobbies, the bias towards having sailing as an interest would not be sufficient for its being picked out as a hobby. Similarly, if millionaire playboys did not have to have jobs none would be picked out. And if the query had been simply "What are Ted's job and hobby?" no contradictory information would have been introduced. The answer, that sailing is

92

Ted's job and he has no hobbies, would be constructed from knowledge in the KB alone. Although no domain constraints are violated in this last case if Ted *does* have a hobby, the system prefers minimal models.

The problem is difficult for two reasons: 1) The search is for an optimal model, rather than a satisficing one, so even if an oracle were available for suggesting a model, it is still hard to verify that it is the best model. 2) The best solution cannot be found by considering the constraints strictly in order of importance, a technique used in prioritized default logic. A model in which Ted's job is corporate raiding and his hobby is TV watching is just as good when only domain constraints are considered. It is the influence of the much weaker minimal model constraints that argues against this model, so constraints of all strengths must be considered at once.

6.4.2   Details of Reasoning Process

When the Lisp interface to the Boltzmann Machine simulator processes the query, the pattern for Ted is clamped into the Subject group, and that for SELF-MADE-MILLIONAIRE-PLAYBOY into the Subject-Type-IO-0 group (see figure 6.5). The pattern for HAS-HOBBY is clamped into the Role-0 group, and HAS-JOB into the Role-1 group. The answer will consist of the objects represented in all the IO groups, but the ones of interest are the Fillers-0 and Fillers-1 groups.

Since Ted is asserted to be a professional sailor in the KB, there are domain constraints built into the Role-Filler-Types group that excite the units $(FILLS \ Has\text{-}Interest \ Sailing)(Ted)$ and $(FILLS \ (RANGE \ Profitable\text{-}Activity) \ Sailing)(Ted)$. Since the $subject = Ted$ unit is on in the Subject group, Ted's features are copied into the Subject-Type group, where these two features will be excited. Similarly, the $(SOME \ Has\text{-}Interest\text{-}TV\text{-}Related\text{-}Activity)(subject)$ unit will be excited because of the assertion that Ted is a TV-BUFF. Simultaneously, the $(SOME \ Has\text{-}Expensive\text{-}Hobby)(subject)$, $(ALL \ Has\text{-}Job \ Armchair\text{-}Activity)(subject)$, and $person(subject)$ units in the Subject-Type group will be excited by the structural constraints between it and the Subject-Type-

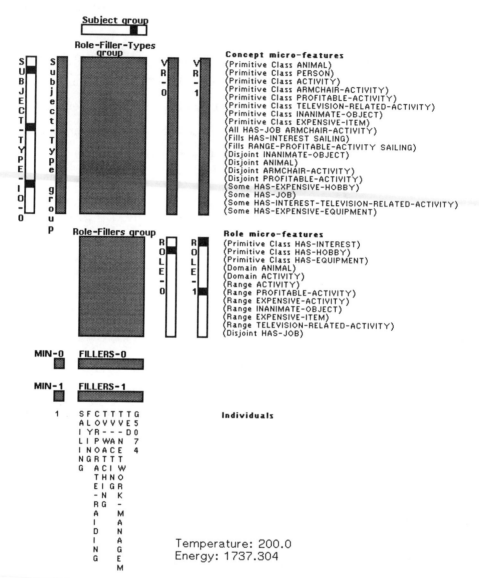

Figure 6.5: Initial state of the network for the example query. The Subject group was clamped to force Ted to be the subject of the query, and the Subject-Type group was clamped to force the subject to be a SELF-MADE-MILLIONAIRE-PLAYBOY. Role-0 was clamped to tell the MINIMUM-FILLERS-0, Fillers-0, and VR-0 groups to pay attention to the HAS-HOBBY role. The pattern for HAS-JOB is clamped into Role-1. Units in all other groups are unclamped, and their state is initialized to one half.

IO-0 group, where SELF-MADE-MILLIONAIRE-PLAYBOY is represented. When these features are copied into the Ted column of the Role-Filler-Types group, they excite the $(SOME\ Has\text{-}Job)(Ted)$ unit. This feature is in turn copied back into the Subject-Type group, where it will exert its influence on Ted's particular role fillers, represented in the Role-Fillers group. Figure 6.6 shows the states of the units at an intermediate stage in the search, where the assertion that Ted's job is sailing is just being overwhelmed by the presupposition that he is a millionaire playboy.

The two units $(FILLS\quad Has\text{-}Interest\quad Sailing)(subject)$ and $(FILLS\ (RANGE\ Profitable\text{-}Activity)\ Sailing)(subject)$ excite the pattern for HAS-JOB in the Sailing column of the Role-Fillers group, that is, the units $has\text{-}interest(subject, Sailing)$ and $(RANGE\ Profitable\text{-}Activity)(subject, Sailing)$. Simultaneously, the $(ALL\ Has\text{-}Job\ Armchair\text{-}Activity)(subject)$ unit activates a constraint that recognizes that Sailing is filling the HAS-JOB role, yet is not an ARMCHAIR-ACTIVITY. This constraint tends to inhibit the pattern for HAS-JOB in the Sailing column. That is, it tries to turn off one of the two units representing HAS-JOB.

The $(SOME\quad Has\text{-}Expensive\text{-}Hobby)(subject)$ unit tries to excite the HAS-EXPENSIVE-HOBBY pattern over some column in the Role-Fillers group. This pattern includes the following features: $(RANGE\ Expensive\text{-}Activity)$ and $has\text{-}hobby$. The former feature will already be active for the individuals Sailing and Flying due to the explicit KB assertions, so it will be easier to assert the pattern for HAS-EXPENSIVE-HOBBY in one of these columns. The other feature of this pattern, $has\text{-}hobby$ tries to excite the $has\text{-}interest$ feature because hobbies are asserted to be interests. But this feature is already somewhat active for Sailing because it is part of the pattern for HAS-JOB. Thus Sailing gets a small head start over Flying, and the system chooses it as Ted's hobby.

It is important that the role HAS-JOB is not atomic. If it were, when the presupposition that Ted is a millionaire playboy results in the system discarding the belief that his job is sailing, there would be no more reason to believe that sailing is any kind of interest. HAS-JOB is in fact defined as an interest that is a profitable activity, so when the system decides it is not profitable in Ted's case, the semantics still prefers models in which Ted is interested in sailing. However the decision to repre-

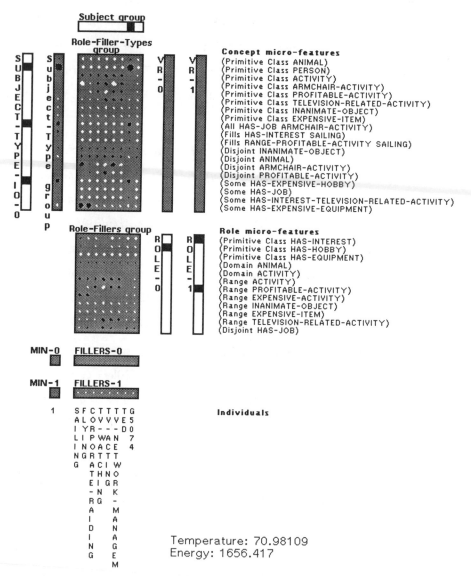

Concept micro-features
(Primitive Class ANIMAL)
(Primitive Class PERSON)
(Primitive Class ACTIVITY)
(Primitive Class ARMCHAIR-ACTIVITY)
(Primitive Class PROFITABLE-ACTIVITY)
(Primitive Class TELEVISION-RELATED-ACTIVITY)
(Primitive Class INANIMATE-OBJECT)
(Primitive Class EXPENSIVE-ITEM)
(All HAS-JOB ARMCHAIR-ACTIVITY)
(Fills HAS-INTEREST SAILING)
(Fills RANGE-PROFITABLE-ACTIVITY SAILING)
(Disjoint INANIMATE-OBJECT)
(Disjoint ANIMAL)
(Disjoint ARMCHAIR-ACTIVITY)
(Disjoint PROFITABLE-ACTIVITY)
(Some HAS-EXPENSIVE-HOBBY)
(Some HAS-JOB)
(Some HAS-INTEREST-TELEVISION-RELATED-ACTIVITY)
(Some HAS-EXPENSIVE-EQUIPMENT)

Role micro-features
(Primitive Class HAS-INTEREST)
(Primitive Class HAS-HOBBY)
(Primitive Class HAS-EQUIPMENT)
(Domain ANIMAL)
(Domain ACTIVITY)
(Range ACTIVITY)
(Range PROFITABLE-ACTIVITY)
(Range EXPENSIVE-ACTIVITY)
(Range INANIMATE-OBJECT)
(Range EXPENSIVE-ITEM)
(Range TELEVISION-RELATED-ACTIVITY)
(Disjoint HAS-JOB)

Individuals

Temperature: 70.98109
Energy: 1656.417

Figure 6.6: Intermediate state of the network for the example query, after searching for 18,000 time steps. In the Subject-Type group, the feature (*ALL Has-Job Armchair-Activity*) prevents the feature (*FILLS* (*RANGE Profitable-Activity*) *Sailing*) from being asserted, enabling sailing to be Ted's hobby rather than his job.

sent only partial models prevents knowledge about role fillers from being represented directly. Instead such information is represented via the creation of complex predicates, such as (*FILLS Has-Job Sailing*). Representing this predicate atomically results in the loss of the ability to represent its being only half true; when the system retracts its belief that sailing is a profitable activity, this predicate becomes false of the subject, and hence there is no more reason the believe the subject has any interest in sailing. To force the system to build two complex predicates, (*FILLS Has-Interest Sailing*) and (*FILLS (RANGE Profitable-Activity) Sailing*), the definition of SAILOR explicitly mentions both of these features (see figure 6.4). This kind of shortcoming of the tractable architecture is one of the reasons μKLONE is intended to be used in familiar domains where the form of the KB can be adjusted until uniformly good performance results.

Choosing Ted's job is the result of three constraints: that all his jobs must be armchair activities, that he must have some television-related interest, and that any job must be a profitable activity. There are two profitable armchair activities, Corporate-Raiding and TV-Network-Management. The constraints on jobs alone do not distinguish between these alternatives. Similarly, Ted's television-related interest could be TV-Watching, TV-Acting, or TV-Network-Management. The constraints that make the system prefer small models lead the system to choosing the single activity in the intersection of these sets, TV-Network-Management, so that only one relationship must be postulated rather than two. Figure 6.7 shows the final state of the network.

6.4.3   Simulation Parameters

The Ted Turner domain includes seven explicitly mentioned individuals. One more made-up individual is added in case some frame requires an individual whose properties do not match any of the seven. The next section gives an example in which the extra individual is made to be an inanimate object in order to fill the HAS-EQUIPMENT role of sailing.

There are eight primitive concept micro-features and ten non-primitive ones. There are three primitive role micro-features and nine non-primitive ones. The network has 266 units in the central groups, and the size of the constraint trees of structural and minimal

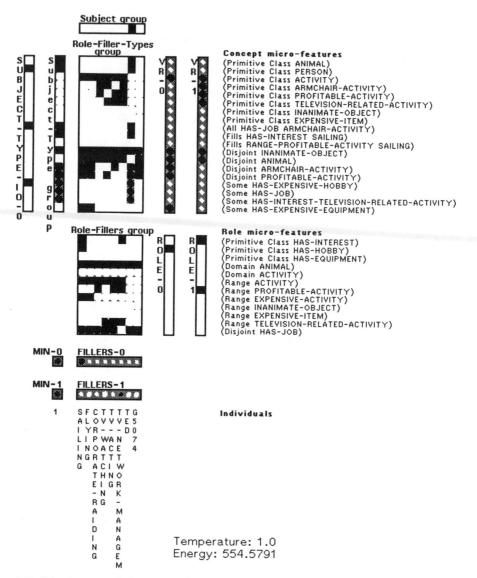

Figure 6.7: Final state of the network for the example query. After the 40,000 steps of the annealing schedule gradually cooling from $T = 200$ to $T = 20$, the temperature was lowered to 1 and the network was run at constant temperature for 1000 time steps. The pattern in MINIMUM-FILLERS-0 means there is at least one filler of the HAS-HOBBY role; the pattern in Fillers-0 means that Sailing is a filler of the HAS-HOBBY role; and the pattern in VR-0 means that all fillers of the HAS-HOBBY role are non-armchair, non-profitable, expensive activities. Similarly for the second set of IO groups, since HAS-JOB was clamped into Role-1, the pattern in MINIMUM-FILLERS-1 means Ted has at least one job; the pattern in Fillers-1 means TV-Network-Management is his job; and the pattern in VR-1 means that all his jobs are armchair, profitable, television-related activities.

98

model constraints is 2817. With one Subject-Type-IO Group, two sets of WITH groups, and a possible argument list to MINIMUM-FILLERS clauses of {1}, there are 96 units in the IO groups. There are a total of 4538 component nodes in the presupposition and complete answer constraint trees.

Although μKLONE uses the Hopfield and Tank search algorithm, which is a deterministic approximation to true simulated annealing, it suffers from similar problems when the temperature is lowered too rapidly. The problem is actually worse, because even with an exponentially long search time the system will not find a global energy minima if the energy space is not sufficiently smooth. Getting good results within a limited time therefore requires some ad hoc parameter tuning. On the other hand, the interaction among minima can lead to beneficial effects that would not accrue if the search randomly sampled from the equilibrium distribution. Section 8.2 describes how this interaction automatically generates prototypes based on the individuals in the KB.

The first time a new domain is defined and a query asked, the answer is unlikely to be correct. The first order problem is a mismatch in the relative weights assigned to structural, domain, and minimal model constraints. Any time there are different weight scales in a network, it is hard to reach equilibrium [White, 1984]. At each temperature, there is a different trade-off between maximizing entropy by assigning equal probabilities to all states, and minimizing energy by assigning the highest probability to low energy states. As the numerical value of the temperature approaches that of the energy difference between two states, the probability ratio between the states begins to increase rapidly. When the temperature decreases slightly more, the higher energy state will effectively be locked out, and the network is said to *freeze*. Constraints with much smaller weights will not have a chance to be considered. This suggests assigning similar weights to structural, domain, and minimal model constraints. Yet if domain constraints are too strong in relation to structural constraints, self-contradictory models may be preferred over merely counterfactual models. Similarly if minimal model constraints are too strong in relation to domain constraints, small models may be preferred over models more consistent with the KB. Since minimal model constraints must be two steps smaller than the strongest constraints, it is especially hard to adjust the weights so that minimal models are usually

99

chosen. This trade-off is different for different domains because the amount of interaction between assertions varies. If the KB contains much unrelated information, the number of domain constraints will be small relative to the number of structural constraints, and the weight scales can be more similar.

The presupposition and complete answer constraints do not pose a problem for reaching equilibrium. As already mentioned, the former are of the same scale as domain constraints. The latter are not supposed to affect the selection of the model, and so do not have to be close in strength to the other constraint types.

By convention, the weight scales are normalized by setting the strongest domain weights to 100. In the Ted Turner domain, structural constraint weights are 300, presupposition weights are 200, domain weights about general knowledge 100, domain weights about particular knowledge 50, minimal model weights are 10, and complete answer weights are 2.

There are two more parameters to be set, the k parameter determining the energy function for IMPLIES constraints, and the p parameter determining the energy function for OR and MAX constraints. For the Ted Turner domain, $k = 1.5$ and $p = 16$. Factors influencing these choices are discussed in section 3.7.2.

Empirically, it seems that the system's behavior is not very sensitive to the value of the structural or presupposition certainties or of k. It is sensitive to the minimal model certainty and p because they strongly influence when commitments are made. A high minimal model certainty requires more "force" to commit to believing a proposition, and delays commitments. A high p distributes most of the force to the leading contender, and results in early commitments. In the Role Shift problem, if p is set too high the system will pick a TV-related interest while it still thinks Ted's job is sailing. Hence there is no motivation to pick a single activity that can be both a job and a TV-related interest. If the minimal model certainty is set too low, there is little resistance to making new assumptions, and the head start that Sailing has as Ted's interest is of little consequence when it comes to choosing his hobby. On the other hand, the disadvantage Sailing has as a prospective hobby due to the fact that hobbies are disjoint from jobs remains the same strength. Thus the system will tend to pick any expensive activity *except* Sailing

100

as Ted's hobby. In fact, the value used for the minimal model certainty is probably higher than one would want for most domains. I have left it there because there is a nice story to tell about slipping from job to hobby. If the minimal model certainty is lowered, and the system chooses flying as Ted's hobby, the decision is still made by interactions among micro-features—those of the roles HAS-EXPENSIVE-HOBBY and HAS-INTEREST and those of the concepts EXPENSIVE-ACTIVITY and PROFITABLE-ACTIVITY. The point of the example is that soft constraints over distributed representations engender plausible reasoning, not that μKLONE understands enough about Ted Turner that it can puzzle out his hobby.

There are other parameters used by the program to govern the search, namely the number of time steps, the temperature at each time step, and the constant determining how fast a unit's derivative is allowed to change its state. If these are set conservatively enough, further changes should not affect the answer. The values used currently, where 40,000 steps are taken in exponentially lowering the temperature from 200 to 20, and where a unit's state is changed by .001 times its derivative, seem to be quite conservative.

A few more degrees of freedom are not used now, but perhaps should be. Currently the energy of a consistent model is non-zero, for two reasons. First, minimal model weights increase the energy of a model in proportion to its size. Second, OR constraints do not perfectly match the mathematical min function. Even when one argument is zero, the energy of the constraint can be positive. These deviations from the ideal mapping from models to energy are pragmatically necessary early in the search to reduce the number of unnecessary assumptions made and to encourage the exploration of several alternative ways to satisfy disjunctions. However once commitments are made to an assumption or a disjunct, these heuristics are just a nuisance. It would be possible to gradually lower the minimal model certainty, and raise the magnitude of p, during search. Then as zero temperature is approached, the measured energy would better reflect the consistency of the model with the KB and presuppositions. At the same time, the certainty of the structural weights could be gradually increased to ensure that the system never ends up with a self-contradictory model, yet allow freedom of exploration early on.

Finally, there is the architecture itself. It is hard to quantify how much the form of the constraints is tuned for the Role Shift problem. I find that I change this almost as often as I change parameter values. On the other hand, all the changes seem to be converging. A year ago there were about 60 parameters to tune instead of just five, and the architecture was far less principled.

The procedure for finding an annealing schedule involves trial and error, but is straightforward. First the starting and ending temperatures are found. A good starting temperature is the lowest one for which all the unit states are close to one half, and a good ending temperature is the highest one for which they are all near zero or one. Next a value for the step size is found. The network is most susceptible to oscillation at low temperatures, so a good value is the largest step size that does not cause oscillation at the ending temperature. Finally, the best number of steps to take is the smallest number such that the network stays close to equilibrium during search. As the temperature is lowered during annealing, the Boltzmann component (see section 3.6) of the energy monotonically decreases. If the system is close to equilibrium, the energy will not change while the system is run at constant temperature. Thus the number of steps is adjusted until pausing the annealing and running at constant temperature does not change the energy much.

With the current annealing schedule, a search takes two days on a Symbolics 3600. While it is easy to predict how the size of the network will scale with the domain, there is as yet little basis for making such a prediction about the number of time steps. In one comparison using an earlier version of μKLONE, some unnecessary information was deleted from the Ted Turner domain. The resulting KB was 34% smaller, yet the annealing schedule could only be shortened by 16%.

6.4.4 Other Queries

The query examined in detail above, "If Ted were a self-made millionaire playboy...?" tests the system's ability to make plausible guesses about role fillers based on the types of the fillers and the similarities between role patterns. This section lists a range of queries about the Ted Turner domain that demonstrate other capabilities.

First several variations on the original query. If the SUBJECT-TYPE clause is left out, eliminating the presupposition that Ted is a millionaire playboy, there are no conflicts to resolve. Ted's job is sailing, and there is no reason to believe he has a hobby. If the presupposition is left out, and the HAS-INTEREST role is asked about, rather than HAS-JOB and HAS-HOBBY, then both sailing and TV-watching are retrieved. Any other TV-related activity would do as well.

Alternatively, parts of the presuppositions can be imposed piecemeal. The query

```
((SUBJECT Ted) (WITH (ROLE Has-Job) (FILLERS ?) (VR Armchair-Activity))
              (WITH (ROLE Has-Interest) (FILLERS ?)))
```

results in retracting the belief that Ted is a professional sailor, just as the original query does, however there is no reason to suppose he has either a hobby or another job in this case. Since Ted is still a TV-Buff, TV-watching is again picked out as an interest.

Asking

```
((SUBJECT Ted)
 (WITH (ROLE Has-Expensive-Hobby) (FILLERS ?) (MINIMUM-FILLERS 1)))
```

forces the model to pick some expensive hobby. A smaller model results when the expensive hobby and the TV-related interest are both the same individual. Thus either flying should be assumed to be a TV-related activity, or some known TV-related activity will be assumed to be an expensive activity. In actual fact, the system assumes that TV-watching is an expensive activity and Ted's hobby. If the user feels that reducing the number of role fillers does not justify making assumptions about the types of individuals, the minimal-model weights used in the Role-Filler-Types group can be raised relative to those in the Role-Fillers group.

So far, the object of all the queries mentioned has been finding out what the fillers of some role are. The query

```
((SUBJECT Ted)
 (SUBJECT-TYPE Self-Made-Millionaire-Playboy)
 (WITH (ROLE ?) (VR Armchair-Activity) (MINIMUM-FILLERS 1)))
```

asks which of Ted's roles are filled only by armchair activities, and should be answered HAS-JOB. However, asking a Role group to actively affect the central groups in response to two conflicting constraints very much exceeds its abilities. The easiest way to satisfy the VR constraint is to turn on all the micro-features, while the easiest way to satisfy the MINIMUM-FILLERS constraint is to turn them all off. It is unable to trade off the constraints sufficiently well, and retrieves HAS-EQUIPMENT

Asking

```
((SUBJECT ?) (SUBJECT-TYPE Professional-Sailor))
```

retrieves Ted. Asking

```
((SUBJECT ?) (SUBJECT-TYPE Expensive-Activity))
```

should retrieve either Sailing or Flying. Flying is chosen because there are fewer assertions about flying, so there are fewer constraints to be imposed on the Subject-Type group. The interesting aspect of this query is that to be an expensive activity requires that the subject have the HAS-EQUIPMENT relation to some EXPENSIVE-ITEM, and there are no individuals in the KB known to meet this description. In fact none of the named individuals can consistently be inanimate objects of any kind. This demonstrates the need for made-up individuals. In this case Dummy is assumed to be an expensive item, and to be in the HAS-EQUIPMENT relation to the subject. The same behavior results from presupposing the definition of EXPENSIVE-ACTIVITY by asking

```
((SUBJECT ?)
 (WITH (ROLE Has-Equipment) (VR Expensive-Item) (MINIMUM-FILLERS 1)))
```

6.4.5   Analysis of Role Shift Problem

The common sense answers to the queries discussed above are given primarily because the representations of roles are distributed across atomic propositions: HAS-JOB generates a pattern of activity similar to that generated by HAS-HOBBY. Since constraints operate over individual units rather than whole roles, roles that share many units have similar properties. Viewed from the level of units, this is not remarkable at all, but symbolic

104

systems that represent roles atomically must have externally specified rules for judging similarity, and such systems must explicitly perform similarity reasoning to get the sort of inexact match achieved here.

The particular answer found is also not critical. There are other reasonable answers that also reflect reasoning by similarity over meaningful patterns. For instance the system could have decided that sailing really is not a VIGOROUS-ACTIVITY, or that SELF-MADE-MILLIONAIRE-PLAYBOY's HAS-JOBs do not have to be ARMCHAIR-ACTIVITYs. In either case Ted's job could be sailing.

The Role Shift problem demonstrates that in spite of the small fraction of a complete model that can be explicitly represented by μKLONE, the system can still do interesting mundane reasoning. There is no limit on the number of factors that can be taken into account in answering a query. In choosing Ted's job, assertions about jobs in general, about millionaire playboy's jobs in particular, and even assertions about Ted's other interests were considered.

The single severe limitation is that contradictions that can only be detected by knowing the role fillers of the subject's role fillers will not be found. For instance if Jaqueline-Kennedy was asserted to be a (SOME Has-Spouse (AND Professional-Sailor Self-Made-Millionaire-Playboy)), the system would happily pick an individual as a filler of the spouse role. Since the contradiction between PROFESSIONAL-SAILOR and SELF-MADE-MILLIONAIRE-PLAYBOY is only apparent upon consideration of the spouse's role-fillers, μKLONE does not detect it. The limitations imposed by the query language guide the user to ask questions that are likely to be appropriate. All clauses in a query must be about one individual, which may be previously known by the system or dynamically created by recruiting a generic made-up individual.

7 Other Connectionist KR Systems

Early semantic networks such as Quillian's [1968] took their graphical representation very seriously, and the meaning of nodes was specified primarily by the spreading activation algorithms defined over various kinds of links. These algorithms were generally parallel and the computations at nodes required only local information. The systems in which nodes pass only activation levels, as opposed to markers, seem very much in keeping with what are now called connectionist nets. Because these networks have the same structure as the user's view of the domain, I call them *isomorphic networks*.

7.1 Isomorphic Systems: Shastri

7.1.1 Overview

Lokendra Shastri's evidential reasoning system [Shastri, 1987] is the most sophisticated isomorphic connectionist KR system developed to date. Figure 7.1 shows some of the information from the Ted Turner domain as a Shastri net. There are two kinds of problems these nets can solve: *inheritance* problems ask the most likely value of some property for some concept—for instance "Is Ted's job more likely to be sailing or flying?" *Classification* problems ask what is the most likely concept given a set of property/value pairs—for instance "Is something whose job is sailing more likely to be a sailor or a TV-buff?" In contrast to NIKL, where queries typically involve subsumption relations, here queries must always involve properties: one would ask whether (Tweety has-mode-of-transport Fly), as opposed to asking whether Tweety is a Flier.

Shastri's KBs contain evidential rather than logical information, and are entirely assertional. For instance the weight on the link from Ted to Sailor indicates the conditional probability of being Ted given that one is a Sailor.[1] On completion of the spreading acti-

---

[1] There can be no exceptions to subsumption relationships, so he computes $\frac{\#ted}{\#sailor}$ rather than $\frac{\#ted \wedge sailor}{\#sailor}$.

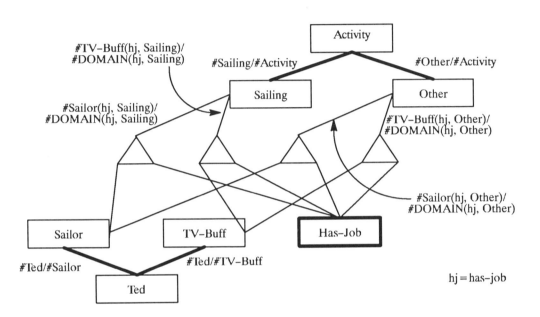

Figure 7.1: Encoding of some of the information about Ted in a Shastri net. The dark rectangle is a property node; other rectangles are concept nodes; triangles are binder nodes (see text). Dark links represent ISA relations and are labeled with conditional probabilities; the labels on other lines represents the distribution of values of a given property for a given concept. This figure is adapted from [Shastri, 1987].

vation algorithm, the relative activation of the various answer nodes reflects the relative conditional probability that each answer is correct. The most active node is chosen as the answer to the query.

In terms of μKLONE's concept-forming constructs, Shastri's system incorporates AND and FILLS. For example the KB can assert that Ted is both a TV-Buff and a Sailor, or that Sailing fills the has-job role of sailors. There are no explicit constructs corresponding to ALL, SOME, or DISJOINT.

Properties are atomic, so there is nothing corresponding to the role-forming constructs DISJOINT and AND. DOMAIN and RANGE declarations are used to constrain the network topology: *binder nodes*, which are shown as triangles in figure 7.1, are built for every (concept1 property concept2) triple such that the distribution of the property for concept1 is known, and concept2 is in the range of the property. Of course the distribution is only defined if concept1 is in the domain of the property. The label on the link connecting a binder node to a value node represents the conditional probability of instantiating concept1 given the value concept2 for the property. In the figure, I have modified Shastri's notation so that #DOMAIN(property value) represents the number of individuals in the domain with the given value for the given property. Shastri uses #value with the consequence that the number of people whose job is sailing, the number of people whose hobby is sailing, and the number of instances of sailing are all written #sailing. Concepts in the range of a property are considered alternative possible values for that property: any given concept is expected to have exactly one of these values for each property it is in the domain of.[2] This implicit mutual exclusion of values allow a weak version of DISJOINT, in that saying (TV-Buff Has-Job Other) implies TV-Buffs' jobs aren't sailing. However Sailing and Other are not considered disjoint in other contexts.

7.1.2   Multiple Views Organization

Shastri nets do Bayesian inference, which is intractable in general. Combining evidence from different sources, which may have complex interdependencies, is responsible for

---

[2]For this reason I keep to Shastri's terminology of properties and values, rather than equating them with roles and fillers.

much of the difficulty. In inheritance graphs, multiple sources of evidence result from multiple ancestors. Shastri has determined a way to quickly combine evidence when only leaf nodes have multiple ancestors. His type hierarchies can thus be thought of as multiple strict hierarchies (trees), which correspond to alternative ways to classify (view) the tokens. For instance, the world can be divided up into living/non-living as well as dangerous/safe. John can then instantiate both living and dangerous.

7.1.3   Types versus Tokens

According to Shastri [Shastri, 1987],

> An agent interprets the world as consisting of instances.... A way of
> structuring the knowledge about the environment is to detect and record
> similarities between objects that occur in the environment. Once recorded,
> these similarities may be exploited to categorize novel objects and to make
> predictions about their properties. Types serve exactly this purpose.

In other words, what we really want to know is assertional knowledge about individuals (taken to exist) in the world. Definitional knowledge functions only to facilitate assertional reasoning. This is the view taken in μKLONE as well.

In Shastri's system, a concept is "a labeled collection of property/value pairs." Although he refers to type concepts and token concepts, they are not distinguished in the representation language. If properties are meant to hold between individuals in the world, then a property value ought to be an individual, rather than a concept. It doesn't make sense to have someone's pet be a labeled collection of property/value pairs. Of course, the species elephant deserves to have properties attached to it, but this should be done with a separate individual—not with the elephant type concept (see figure 7.2). Although values are allowed to be any concept, all Shastri's examples use token concepts. There is nothing to prevent Shastri from changing his representation language so that types and tokens are distinguished in the input, and doing type checking to ensure that only tokens can be values. It would be a helpful clarification.

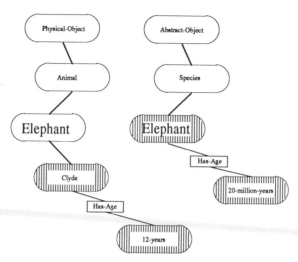

Figure 7.2: Illustration of the need for a distinction between types and tokens. The type elephant is merely a computational fiction, used to cache properties of instances. The token elephant can be a value of properties, and can have property values, but these should not be inherited by instances of elephants. For instance, Clyde should not inherit the property value has-age/20-million-years. Shaded ovals are individuals, other ovals are concepts, rectangles are roles. Heavy lines are ISA links.

7.1.4 Evaluation

Shastri's system provably finds the most probable value, or most probable concept, very quickly—in time proportional to the depth of the concept hierarchy. However he pays a price in expressive power. At the language level, the missing constructs result from the assumption of one value per property, and from the primitiveness of properties. A more severe restriction is that the concept hierarchy must be rather tree-like, and that the possible answers to a query must be disjoint from the concepts activated in posing the query. If the domain and range of a property overlap, care is needed to prevent crosstalk. These restrictions can all be traced to the the problem of binding. Although binder nodes unambiguously stand for a (subject, relation, object) triple, much as Role-Fillers units in μKLONE, they must communicate via concept nodes. There is only one Ted node in the network, and it becomes active whether Ted is the subject or the value of any property. For properties with non-overlapping domains and ranges, the ambiguity can be resolved. If has-job is active, and Ted is active, it must be because Ted has the job. Since this organization prevents interaction among properties, the interesting

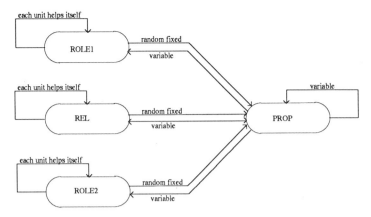

Figure 7.3: The architecture of Hinton's connectionist implementation of semantic networks. The ROLE1 and ROLE2 groups use identical micro-feature representations of concepts. The REL group uses a different micro-feature representation of relations. The PROP units are not semantically interpretable. This figure is taken from [Hinton, 1981].

counterfactual consequences of Ted's being a millionaire playboy could never be explored. Although it may be possible to do some sort of chaining in Shastri's nets, any such chain would have to thread its way through disjoint sets of concepts, and could never double back, so it could not do anything μKLONE couldn't by sequential queries.

7.2 Register Systems

7.2.1 Hinton's Semantic Nets

Hinton [1981] introduces a profligate solution to the binding problem, which is essentially the one μKLONE uses: One isomorphic network is built for every individual that must be simultaneously represented. Each isomorphic network contains a unit for every feature the individuals may have, and links between the units ensure that the final state of the units represents a complete and consistent description of the individual. The links no longer have a knowledge level interpretation, such as ISA or Has-Color. The overall architecture is determined by the syntax of triples—not by the user's domain theory. I call this kind of architecture a *register network*. In Hinton's system there are three registers: ROLE1 represents an individual, REL represents a property of that individual, and ROLE2 represents the value of the property. Given a value for any two registers as input, the system fills in the third. Figure 7.3 shows the architecture of his system.

Hinton uses perceptron units, which sum the weights from active input units and become active themselves if and only if the sum exceeds a threshold [Minsky and Papert, 1969]. It is impossible to effect arbitrary functions from two registers to one register with perceptrons. However with the introduction of "hidden units" whose states are unconstrained by the task itself, any mapping is possible. The PROP module contains hidden units, and its only function is to ensure that the correct pattern is filled in as the missing element of the triple. The random fixed weights from the three registers produce a patterns of activation in the PROP module independent of the domain theory. The variable weights are trained using the perceptron convergence procedure from examples of triples that hold in the domain. For each PROP pattern resulting from one of these triples, the weights to each register are trained to reproduce the element of the triple in that register, and the PROP pattern is trained to reproduce itself. After training, three properties hold [Hinton, 1981]:

1. Any two components of a triple would cause states of the PROP assembly similar to the state that represented the complete triple.

2. States of the PROP assembly that were similar to a state representing a complete triple would cause subsequent states even more similar to the state representing that triple.

3. A state of the PROP assembly representing a particular triple would cause the appropriate states of the ROLE1, REL, and ROLE2 assemblies.

After several cycles, the system would converge to a complete triple. This scheme for making correct triples stable states of the system was designed before the concept of energy minimization in networks was discovered. The goal is just the same as that of the Hopfield and Tank algorithm in μKLONE.

Hinton also introduced an economy in the representation of the types of individuals that makes the process of inheritance an emergent property. Concept units are built not for every distinguishable concept, but for all the primitives from which the concepts are defined. Then any concept can be represented by some pattern of activation over these *micro-features*. The pattern of activity over a set of micro-feature units is called a

112

distributed representation of a concept [Hinton *et al.*, 1986]. The pattern for more specific concepts includes the patterns for their subsumers, so no spreading activation is needed to ensure that the ISA hierarchy is respected. He does not describe a systematic method for choosing features, but simply makes up patterns in which similar individuals have similar patterns. It would be possible to use μKLONE's algorithm to find patterns for the entities in Hinton's system.

Instead of compiling the distributed representations from a high level language, Hinton chose in a later paper to learn the representations as well as the relations. Hinton [1986] demonstrates that appropriate micro-features can be learned. He presented the network with triples representing family relationships, such as (John Has-Father Bob). The triples exhibited regularities, such as the fact that if the second element is Has-Father, then the third element must be male. By limiting the capacity of the network so that it must exploit the regularities in order to correctly fill in missing arguments, the network is made to develop representations of the individuals that include micro-features that correspond to sex, age, and branch of the family.

In the 1981 paper Hinton anticipated the use of conjunctive coding to represent the cross product of role features with concept features. Rather than having discrete registers for different roles, he proposes that similar roles might share units, allowing emergent inheritance of roles and fine distinctions between roles.

Using registers, there is no interference between the two individuals simultaneously represented, so there is no need for the "multiple views" restriction on the KB. On the other hand, Hinton still does not distinguish between concepts and individuals, and he cannot represent multiple fillers of a role. Since only one triple can be represented at a time, rather than a whole frame, interactions between roles cannot be investigated, nor is chaining possible.

μKLONE is a direct development of this system. It introduces individuals as distinct from concepts, so that they can be represented with a single unit, rather than as a set of features. Groups representing role fillers consist of individual units rather than feature units, so sets of role fillers can be represented. To enable this to work, there must be a table of individual types stored elsewhere. In addition, μKLONE implements Hinton's suggestion of feature-based representations for roles, so inheritance of fillers up the role hierarchy becomes an emergent feature of the architecture. Among the register networks, only μKLONE has a knowledge-level formal semantics.

7.2.2   McClelland and Kawamoto

McClelland and Kawamoto [1986] present a system that learns to transform the surface structure of example sentences into a deep structure representation. It has eight distinct groups of units. Four represent surface cases and four represent deep cases. In the groups representing surface cases, a two dimensional distributed representation is used in which each unit represents the conjunction of a pair of features of the case filler, so there is emergent inheritance up the type hierarchy for each case filler. In the groups representing deep cases, a two dimensional conjunctive representation is again used, but the units in these groups represent the conjunction of a feature of the verb of the sentence and a feature of the case filler. Here there is emergent inheritance up the type hierarchy for each case filler and simultaneously up the type hierarchy for verbs. This system comes the closest to μKLONE's simultaneous concept and role inheritance. Although McClelland and Kawamoto have simultaneous inheritance over verbs and fillers, they represent each role filler in a different group of units, precluding their inheritance from one role to another.

Of all the connectionist systems using distributed representations to achieve inheritance and fine gradations of meaning over structured knowledge, McClelland and Kawamoto are most serious about their application. They suggest that their method of concurrent syntactic and semantic interpretation, their treatment of ambiguity, and their incorporation of defaults and context dependencies offer advantages over symbolic sentence processing theories. Because language understanding is such an important aspect of mundane reasoning, the next chapter includes a section outlining how the performance (but of course not the learning) of McClelland and Kawamoto's system could be emulated using μKLONE.

In later work, McClelland has concentrated on learning the internal representations not only of the nouns and verbs, but also of the role structures themselves [John and

114

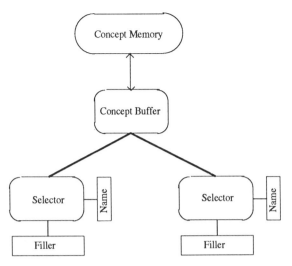

Figure 7.4: The DUCS architecture. This figure is taken from [Touretzky and Geva, 1987].

McClelland, 1988]. However, the scheme developed by the network for encoding sentence structure is not yet well understood, and so the later work has less to say about issues of representation.

7.2.3 DUCS

DUCS [Touretzky and Geva, 1987] is an outgrowth of μKLONE with a similar mechanism for concept and role inheritance. The topology and weights in the network are domain-independent, and the focus of the research is on sequential reasoning. As in Shastri's system, a concept is a set of slot/filler pairs, and each slot can have only one value. This allows DUCS to have distributed representations for fillers. Again, there is no distinction between individuals and concepts. In figure 7.4, each Name/Filler pair is analogous to a Role-n/Fillers-n pair of I/O groups in μKLONE, and serve to specify or recall a subset of the slot/filler pairs that constitute a concept. The selector groups are hidden units that facilitate combining or extracting distinct slot/filler pairs from the complete representation of the concept in the concept buffer. If μKLONE used only pairwise links, as DUCS does, it would also require a selector group associated with each set of I/O groups.

The mapping from slot/filler patterns to selector group patterns is not the simple conjunctive coding used in μKLONE, but is designed to produce an essentially random pattern. This has the advantages that there is less crosstalk among semantically similar slot/filler pairs and that the size of the selector groups and concept buffer grow only as $O(n)$ rather than $O(n^2)$. In μKLONE the regular mapping produces semantically meaningful units in the Role-Fillers group, so the compiler can effect the domain knowledge. For instance, a Role-Fillers unit may stand for the conjunction of the role micro-feature ($RANGE$ $Activity$) and the individual sailing, and it is easy to enforce this semantics by building an IMPLIES constraint from this unit to the unit meaning that sailing is an activity. Since a DUCS network contains no domain-specific knowledge in its connections, it can be built by hand even without having semantically interpretable units.

The concept buffer is isomorphic to the selector groups, and a concept buffer unit is active if and only if at least one of the corresponding selector group units is active. Thus the representation of a concept in the concept buffer is the inclusive OR of the representations for the slot/filler pairs. This is similar to the ORing of inputs from different role I/O groups in μKLONE in the Role-Fillers group, except that in μKLONE the result is not considered the complete representation of the concept.

The concept memory is a Willshaw associative memory [Willshaw, 1981], which can store many complete concept patterns. To retrieve a concept from a partial specification, the partial concept pattern is first assembled in the concept buffer from the selector groups representing known name/filler pairs. Using associative recall from concept memory, this pattern is completed, and the desired slot fillers can then be read out of the unclamped fillers groups.

Since DUCS' knowledge is represented in states rather than constraints, it is capable of recursive and sequential reasoning tasks impossible for μKLONE. The concept "Bill knows that John kissed Mary"[3] requires the embedded concept "John kissed Mary" to fill one of the slots. Although μKLONE can have individuals of any sort filling slots, they have to be pre-defined in the KB. It is much better to be able to construct a representation for structured individuals like this example on the fly. In DUCS, a hashing function maps

---

[3]This would be an individual in μKLONE terminology.

the complete pattern for a concept onto a much smaller pattern for a slot filler. This mapping does not maintain semantic information, so can not be used in conjunction with micro-feature based filler patterns. It does meet the important requirement that the representation of the complex whole can be used to associatively retrieve the complete concept pattern from the Willshaw memory. Once retrieved, the full pattern for "John kissed Mary" can be decomposed into its component slot/filler pairs.

Secondly, inference can be performed in the concept memory. For instance training from examples could be used to learn the script default "If x enters a restaurant, and x orders food, then x eats the food."

7.2.4 Dolan

For his thesis [Dolan, 1989], Dolan has built a system for storing and retrieving schemas, which are more expressive than concepts. While a concept consists of restrictions on roles and fillers, all of which apply to a single individual, a schema may involve multiple individuals, each of which has different restrictions on its roles and fillers. Therefore every schema restriction must explicitly specify all three components of a (individual1 role individual2) triple. For instance, in the restaurant schema the food eaten by the customer must be the same food brought by the waiter. This is expressed by using the same variable in different triples: ($ingest actor $customer), ($ingest object $food), ($ptrans actor $waiter), ($ptrans object $food), ($ptrans to $customer). On a particular occasion if Willy waiter brings Clyde customer some Fries, we know (ptrans23 actor willy), (ptrans23 object fries), and (ptrans23 to clyde), and can then infer (ingest14 actor clyde) and (ingest14 object fries).

Dolan's system stores schemas in long term memory. When it is presented with a subset of instantiated triples in short-term memory, it extracts the best-matching variablized schema from long term memory and activates all its triples in a retrieval buffer (see figure 7.5). These are mapped back onto short term memory, where they constitute a complete instantiated schema. The mapping units ensure that each variable that occurs in triples in the retrieval buffer is always mapped to the same individual in short term memory.

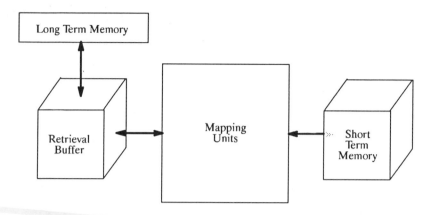

Figure 7.5: Dolan's network architecture. The Retrieval Buffer and Short Term Memory are drawn as cubes to indicate that conjunctive coding is used. ROLE1 micro-features are laid out along the z axis, ROLE2 micro-features along the x axis, and REL micro-features along the y axis. The pattern for a triple is the cross product of the three feature vectors, just as the pattern for a pair in μKLONE's Role-Filler-Types groups is the cross product of two vectors. This figure is adapted from [Dolan and Dyer, 1988].

By using explicit variables to implement coreference constraints, Dolan incurs the cost of a rather complicated mapping scheme. In contrast, Role Value Maps in μKLONE perform the same function with conditional equality constraints. If the has-friends of deadbeats are the same as the has-creditors, then a *has-friends=has-creditors* concept micro-feature is built that activates the equality constraint. Of course the μKLONE constraint has to be "compiled" in, while Dolan's mapping units "interpret" the variables in the schema on the fly, so his method is much more flexible. In addition more complexity is required in his case because he must map triples rather than pairs. Although he is forced to use an awkward variable binding mechanism that would be be much simpler in a symbolic system, he benefits from the connectionist settling algorithm for finding the best match, which would be awkward to implement in a symbolic system.

By moving to schemas rather than concepts, Dolan can handle the problem of chaining. Except for long term memory, the network topology and weights are domain independent. However he still cannot have variable numbers of role fillers, because the triples in the retrieval buffer must match those in short term memory one-to-one. And the conception of schemas being simply sets of triples is rather limited—there are no ALL, DISJOINT, SOME, DOMAIN, or RANGE restrictions. Lacking this expressive power, counter-

118

factual information cannot have interesting consequences for other beliefs.

Further, schemas are still not as powerful as scripts, which also include causal relations or at least temporal sequences. Dolan's example, the restaurant schema, suffers from the lack of any causal relationship between the customer ordering food and the waiter bringing it.

7.3 Summary

	Dolan	μKLONE	DUCS	M&K	Shastri	Hinton
Organizing Principle	schema	frame	frame	frame	frame	triple
Construction Method	hand	compiled	hand	learned	compiled	learned
Interpretable Units	•	•	some	•	•	some
Concept Inheritance		•	1	•	•	•
Role Inheritance		•	1			
Multiple Fillers		•				
Chaining	•					
Recursive Representations			2			
Guaranteed Correct					•	
Complexity (space × time)	$n^4 \times ?$	$n^3 \times ?$	$n^2 \times ?$	$n^4 \times 1$	$n^3 \times 1$	$n^2 \times ?$

Notes:

1. Similar slots and similar fillers have similar patterns,
but subsumption is no different from other kinds of similarity.

2. Dynamically created nested fillers do not have interpretable patterns,
and do not respect the similarity metric referred to in note 1.

The table above summarizes the characteristics of the six connectionist KR systems discussed in this section. It is arranged in approximately reverse chronological order, which generally corresponds to decreasing grain size, and decreasing time and space complexity. Shastri and μKLONE nets are compiled from a high level language, and have a knowledge-level semantics. Strictly speaking, it is only for these two that it is meaningful to say whether answers are guaranteed to be correct. McClelland and Kawamoto's nets, as well as Hinton's, have their topology specified by the designer, but the weights are learned from examples. Dolan and DUCS nets are entirely constructed by hand. In DUCS and Hinton nets only the input/output units have concise knowledge-level interpretations. The mapping to other units are complex, resulting in uninterpretable hidden units. Concept inheritance is done explicitly via control units in Shastri's nets, and emergently in the others through the use of micro-features. In DUCS, however, all patterns have the same number of bits on, so the pattern for a superconcept cannot be a subset of the pattern for a subconcept. This prevents it from distinguishing similarities due to subsumption from other kinds of similarity. μKLONE is the only system to distinguish concepts from individuals, and hence the only system that can represent multiple role fillers. It is only by having atomic representations of individuals that distributed representations of sets of individuals are disambiguated. Only Dolan can do chaining, because only he can simultaneously represent multiple frames simultaneously. Only DUCS can dynamically create a representation of an individual instance of a structured concept, although the mapping from concept to individual does not respect any micro-feature interpretation the designer might have attributed to patterns in the Name groups. For calculating the space and time complexity of the networks as a function of the KB size, the KB size, n, is defined as the sum of the number of concepts, roles, and individuals for the isomorphic nets, and as the sum of the number of concept, role, and individual features for the register nets. The complexity is as the size of the corresponding network (units plus links) times the retrieval time assuming the network was actually implemented as a parallel machine. Only the order of the asymptotically dominant terms are given, so n^3 means $O(n^3)$. For the systems whose search algorithms involve settling, the times are not given because there is no tight analytic bound. The empirical evidence from μKLONE suggests a time complexity of $O(n)$.

120

8 Open Questions

8.1 Reduced Descriptions

μKLONE represents concepts and roles as sets of features, so assertions can be tied directly to relevant aspects of the model. This reduces the computational overhead that would be involved if terms were represented as atomic symbols only used to access data structures containing the features. In particular, there need be no "inheritance" algorithm to look up the ISA hierarchy and find features. But conventional implementations of knowledge representation systems can and do use sets to represent terms internally [Pigman, 1984], [Marc Vilain, personal communication]. And since μKLONE's features are the same as those consulted in conventional implementations, there is no knowledge-level advantage to its use of distributed representations.

Yet connectionists seem to believe that distributed representations have the potential, at least, to be functionally different from symbolic representations [Hinton *et al.*, 1986]. By symbolic representations, or "local representations," is meant that each unit can be given a reasonably concise meaning in the same terms that the user uses to describe the domain. In μKLONE the meaning of each unit is an atomic proposition in which the predicates are taken directly from the user's domain description. In contrast, DCPS [Touretzky and Hinton, 1985] stores triples of letters using units that stand for unnatural predicates, such as "a triple in which the first element is one of {b j m t v y}, the second element is one of {c f o r u w} and the third is one of {a e g m q x}."

One interpretation of the significance of μKLONE is that there is no fundamental difference between local representations and distributed, uninterpretable representations. μKLONE's architecture is similar to previous connectionist systems that have used distributed representations or coarse coding, with the major difference being that their features were chosen randomly, and μKLONE's are created algorithmically from a high level domain description. What could possibly be the advantage of having no basis for

121

the choice of features? Aside from more compact representations of triples, DCPS and BoltzCons [Touretzky, 1986a] get no functional advantage from their unnatural representations. DUCS [Touretzky and Geva, 1987] has demonstrated the ability to slip between roles in answering questions involving contradictory knowledge, but the same kind of capability was demonstrated for μKLONE.

Although no knowledge representation system to date has demonstrated functionality beyond that achieved by μKLONE by virtue of using non-symbolic representations, I think this will not remain true for long. Access to complex structures from small fixed-size objects is of fundamental importance in computer science. Symbols are the most common way to accomplish this, but they have only an arbitrary relation to the structures they designate. Hash codes are a way to form finite objects from complex structures in a well-defined way, but the goal has generally been to make the relationship as obscure as possible, so that similar structures will have *different* representations. In document retrieval, signature files are composed of hash functions from segments of text to a set of features, and the goal is to make similar documents have similar encodings. Then good guesses can be made as to which documents are appropriate to a query without having to examine the document itself. As with μKLONE's term features, the signature features have a natural description at the level of the user's domain description, and the representations are guaranteed to preserve certain properties.

μKLONEs features only preserve properties that are explicitly mentioned in the KB. For instance the Ted Turner KB uses the clause (SOME Has-Job), so this indirect property is made a concept feature. But there is no feature (SOME Has-Hobby). It would be nice if all the information that could be looked up about an individual was directly represented in its type, but in general this is impractical. One particular kind of information that would be especially useful was pointed out by Ron Brachman (personal communication). The part-of relation is semi-transitive, so some information about parts of parts would be useful. The top level parts of a car are things like engines and wheels. But if the query is "What part of a car is a valve?" a valve of the engine of the car makes a good guess in the absence of any top level component valves.

Hinton [1988] suggests that a term representation should include features of all the

122

role-fillers at a reduced level of detail. Hence he calls these representations "reduced descriptions." Since the role filler's properties will in turn include properties of their role fillers, the result is conceptually an infinite tree of frames at ever lower levels of detail, stored in a finite object. And since role chains can be cyclic, somewhere down in the tree will be another copy of the whole structure. Jordan Pollack (personal communication) has suggested using fractal functions to generate representations. Less far-fetched, David Ackley (personal communication) and Jordan Pollack [1988] have used connectionist networks to learn flat representations from which trees can be reconstructed.

8.2 Prototypes

In the description of μKLONE's reasoning about Ted's being a millionaire playboy, the process of choosing his hobby was explained in terms of the dynamics of unit activations rather than energy. Yet the purpose of using a Boltzmann Distribution is that process-independent explanations can be given. In this case, however, finding the desired answer cannot be explained in energy terms, because sailing would not be preferred over flying if an equilibrium distribution were reached. In both cases one domain constraint is violated: that Ted has the feature ($FILLS$ $has\text{-}job$ $Sailing$). The size of the model is the same in each case. However there are two classes of plausible models where Ted has an interest in sailing; those in which it fills the hobby requirement of millionaire playboys, and those in which it fills the job requirement of professional sailors. The system tends to get in a state that is a superposition of these two classes of models as it tries to satisfy as many constraints as possible. The result of superposition is dynamic creation of prototypes, or combinations of features common to many of the individuals being "considered." The system is most likely to make assumptions compatible with these prototypes. Since the two states are fundamentally at odds, the system cannot go on killing two birds with one stone forever, but once the common elements are activated, the system is more likely to choose a model compatible with these unit states than an equally good alternative, flying, which is more distant in state space.

This is a marginal example of reasoning using prototypes. Models in which Ted is interested in sailing are more typical of the situations described in the query (including both the model chosen and less likely models in which Ted really is a professional sailor) than models in which Ted is interested in flying. A better example involves queries that do not specify a subject. For instance if the query ((SUBJECT-TYPE Activity)) is asked, without any other context, then each known activity is an equally good answer in terms of energy. In this domain, three of the six known activities are asserted to be profitable activities, and only one is asserted not to be. As the system searches over activities, everything else being equal, half the time the *Profitable-Activity* unit in the Subject-Type group will be activated, and only a sixth of the time will it be inhibited. Once the unit becomes excited, there is a process of positive feedback. TV-Watching is less likely to be selected, because of the activity of the *profitable-activity(subject)* unit, so this feature becomes even less likely to receive inhibition. Once *profitable-activity(subject)* is firmly on, activities that are known to have the feature become more likely than those than merely may have it. In order to match the pattern in the Subject-Type group, the latter activities must activate the feature in their column of the Role-Filler-Types group, increasing the size of the model. The former activities, however, would already have this feature active. The system tends to pick activities that are prototypical of all the activities it knows about. McClelland [1981] has previously described prototype extraction from knowledge about particular individuals due to positive feedback from a feature set to the individuals having the features.

8.3 Reducing Space Complexity

One of μKLONE's disadvantages is that the size of the constraints grows as the cube of the KB size. However most of these units represent propositions with "type errors," such as *activity(Ted)*. Thinking of the KB in graphical terms, it is a rooted directed acyclic graph. Each frame in the graph can be expected to be associated with a constant number of new features, so the number of features can be expected to grow linearly with the KB. Yet the number of features an individual has would grow with the height of the tree, $O(\log n)$. The number of units grows with the square of the number of features,

124

but the number of active units will only grow as $O(\log^2 n)$. Thus there is a great waste of processing power using the straightforward encoding in terms of the cross product of all the knowledge-level features. Perhaps by learning sets of features appropriate to a particular domain, this potential complexity reduction can be realized. Unfortunately, in the resulting network there might be no neat rows and columns, but rather a coarse coded jumble of unintelligible units. Also, eliminating units standing for propositions with type errors would prevent some kinds of counterfactual reasoning. One would not want the knowledge that Sailing is a vigorous activity to result in the elimination of the unit *armchair-activity(Sailing)*. Perhaps type errors could be enforced down to the basic category level [Brown, 1958]. Basic categories are the most abstract concepts that people can form a mental image of. For instance dog is a basic category because people can imagine a generic dog that isn't any specific breed. Further, they cannot image generic instances of more abstract categories such as mammal.

8.4 Sentence Processing

Of all the mundane tasks that people carry out, language use has been the most widely studied in artificial intelligence. In fact the most agreed-upon test of intelligence, the Turing Test, is a test of the ability to use language. Natural languages are surprisingly hard to formalize. It is now known that just to reproduce stories in another language requires tremendous amounts of world and cultural knowledge, as well as linguistic knowledge of both literal and idiomatic uses of words. Since language understanding requires much the same knowledge as non-linguistic understanding, it stands to reason that a KR system good for one will be good for the other.[1]

The sentence processing paradigm used here originates with Fillmore [1968], whose work also influenced the development of frame-based knowledge representation systems. In this conception, each clause in a natural language sentence is mapped to a *case frame*, each having a number of *cases*. Case frames are analogous to concepts in μKLONE, and cases are analogous to roles. The clause's main verb determines the type of case frame.

---

[1]Lakoff [1987] presents a mountain of evidence that the same conceptual structures underlie language understanding and other aspects of cognition.

Fillmore hoped that a small number of cases would suffice to categorize the semantic role each syntactic constituent played in the clause. Some of the cases he introduced are:

agent The actor performing the action specified by the verb.

patient The object being acted upon by the agent.

instrument An intermediary between agent and patient.

The sentence is considered understood if the correct mapping from syntactic cases (subject, direct object, and indirect object) to semantic cases is found.

8.4.1   Task Description

As an illustration, this section outlines how the task of assigning roles to sentence constituents examined by McClelland and Kawamoto [1986] could be carried out using μKLONE. Input to their system consists of up to four syntactic constituents. There is a Subject-NP,[2] a Verb, and an optional Object-NP. If the Object-NP is present there may also be a With-NP, a prepositional phrase introduced by "with" that is either an instrument or a modifier of the patient of the action. Some examples are:

The bat moved.

The window broke.

The hammer hit the rock.

The man ate the spaghetti with the cheese.

The man ate the spaghetti with the fork.

The output of the system assigns each NP to one of the following cases: Agent, Patient, Instrument, or Modifier. In addition, ambiguities in the verb and the NPs are resolved. For instance in the sentence "The bat moved," "bat" is interpreted as the mammal rather than the sports equipment. "Move" is interpreted as requiring a "doer," as opposed to its meaning in "The rock moved." And bat is assigned the case agent.

---

[2]NP stands for "noun phrase," for example "the man."

McClelland and Kawamoto train their network from examples of correct input/output pairs. The examples are each generated from one of nineteen rules. In this section I will only mention four of their rules, the four that generate sentences using the verb "hit."

1. The HUMAN hitAVP the THING.

2. The HUMAN hitAVPM the HUMAN with the POSSESSION.

3. The HUMAN hitAVPI the THING with the HITTER.

4. The HITTER hitIVP the THING.

"HitAVP," (for hit-Agent-Verb-Patient) refers to the sense of "hit" in which the Subject-NP is the Agent, the (syntactic) verb is the (case) verb, and the Object-NP is the Patient. Each noun category in a rule is replaced by any noun of the appropriate type to generate a sentence. The following table lists some of the substitutions that can be used in these four rules.

Noun Category	Instances
HUMAN	man, woman, boy, girl
THING	*everything*
POSSESSION	ball, dog, bb-bat, doll, hatchet, hammer, vase
HITTER	ball, bb-bat, hammer

"bb-bat" means the baseball sense of bat. In all cases of ambiguity, the input representation is ambiguous (the average of the representations for the different senses of "bat"), but the output representation must be complete (eg, bb-bat).

8.4.2 μKLONE Implementation

To represent the task in μKLONE, the four syntactic constituents are mapped to four different roles, and the five cases are mapped to five different roles. Since the syntactic verb is always the same as the case verb, one μKLONE role can do double duty, making a total of eight roles. Figure 8.1 shows the role definitions.

Each noun category is made a concept, and each noun is made an individual (figure 8.3). To account for the micro-feature representation of nouns and verbs, more

```
;;;Define the four syntactic category roles
(DEFROLE Has-Syntactic-Constituent (PRIMITIVE))
(DEFROLE Has-Subject-NP (PRIMITIVE))
(DEFROLE Has-Object-NP (PRIMITIVE))
(DEFROLE Has-With-NP (PRIMITIVE))
(DEFROLE Has-Verb (PRIMITIVE))
(ROLE-COVER 100 Has-Syntactic-Constituent
  Has-Subject-NP Has-Object-NP Has-With-NP Has-Verb)

;;;Define the five case roles (verb is shared)
(DEFROLE Has-Semantic-Constituent (PRIMITIVE))
(DEFROLE Has-Agent (PRIMITIVE))
(DEFROLE Has-Patient (PRIMITIVE))
(DEFROLE Has-Instrument (PRIMITIVE))
(DEFROLE Has-Modifier (PRIMITIVE))
(ROLE-COVER 100 Has-Syntactic-Constituent
  Has-Agent Has-Patient Has-Instrument Has-Modifier Has-Verb)
```

Figure 8.1: The inputs and outputs of the role-assignment task are all assigned a μKLONE role. It is convenient to also define two more abstract categories, the syntactic roles and the semantic ones. To express the fact that any syntactic role must be one of its four subcategories, the ROLE-COVER assertion is used. It is defined in figure 8.2.

The macro (CONCEPT-COVER $certainty$ $superconcept$ $c_1 \cdots c_n$) is an abbreviation for the following two assertions:

```
(ASSERT-CONCEPT certainty (OR c₁···cₙ) superconcept)
(ASSERT-CONCEPT certainty
      (AND (DISJOINT c₁) ··· (DISJOINT cₙ)) (DISJOINT superconcept))
```

The macro (CONCEPT-PARTITION $certainty$ $superconcept$ $c_1 \cdots c_n$) is an abbreviation for the following set of assertions:

```
(CONCEPT-COVER certainty superconcept c₁···cₙ)

(ASSERT-CONCEPT certainty c₁ (DISJOINT (OR c₂···cₙ)))
(ASSERT-CONCEPT certainty c₂ (DISJOINT (OR c₁ c₃···cₙ)))
···
(ASSERT-CONCEPT certainty cₙ (DISJOINT (OR c₁···cₙ₋₁)))
```

Similar definitions hold for ROLE-COVER and ROLE-PARTITION.

Figure 8.2: Macro definitions for the assertions COVER and PARTITION. In set theory, $s_1 \cdots s_n$ are said to *cover* S if and only if $\bigcup_{i=1}^{n} s_i = S$, and are said to *partition* S if and only if they cover S and are pairwise disjoint.

```
;;;Define the categories used by rules
(DEFCONCEPT Thing)
(DEFCONCEPT Possession (PRIMITIVE))
(DEFCONCEPT Hitter (PRIMITIVE))
(DEFCONCEPT Human (PRIMITIVE))

(INSTANTIATE-CONCEPT 100 Human Man)
(INSTANTIATE-CONCEPT 100 (AND Hitter Possession) Ball)
```

Figure 8.3: The categories used by the sentence generation rules are defined as concepts, and the possible substitutions are instances of those concepts.

concepts are defined. For instance each noun can be categorized along the gender dimension as either male, female, or neuter (figure 8.4). The effect of assigning nouns to sets of these concepts is creating micro-feature patterns similar to those McClelland and Kawamoto use, with the addition of micro-features for the clauses like (DISJOINT Male).

Finally, each sentence-forming rule can be made a concept, too. The definition expresses the constraints on the input roles, and an assertion expresses the constraints on the output roles (figure 8.5). In addition, there are global assertions that apply to all sentences, such as the fact that the fillers of all the syntactic roles must also be fillers of semantic roles (why else would they be there?).

The following query would extract the role assignments for the sentence "The man hit the woman:"

```
(QUERY '((WITH (ROLE Has-Subject-NP) (FILLERS Man))
         (WITH (ROLE Has-Verb) (FILLERS Hit))
         (WITH (ROLE Has-Object-NP) (FILLERS Woman))
         (WITH (ROLE Has-Agent) (FILLERS ?) (VR ?))
         (WITH (ROLE Has-Patient) (FILLERS ?) (VR ?))
         (WITH (ROLE Has-Instrument) (FILLERS ?) (VR ?))
         (WITH (ROLE Has-Modifier) (FILLERS ?) (VR ?))
         (WITH (ROLE Has-Verb) (VR ?))))
```

For the output roles, the FILLERS clauses specify what nouns fill each case, and the VR

```
;;;Define the micro-features
(DEFCONCEPT Male (PRIMITIVE))
(DEFCONCEPT Female (PRIMITIVE))
(DEFCONCEPT Neuter (PRIMITIVE))

(DEFCONCEPT Doer (PRIMITIVE))
(DEFCONCEPT Non-Doer (PRIMITIVE))

(DEFCONCEPT Noun (PRIMITIVE))
(CONCEPT-PARTITION 100 Noun
  Male Female Neuter)

(DEFCONCEPT Verb (PRIMITIVE))
(CONCEPT-PARTITION 100 Verb
  Doer Non-Doer)

(INSTANTIATE-CONCEPT 100 Male Man)
(INSTANTIATE-CONCEPT  40 Doer Hit)
```

Figure 8.4: In order to include the representations used by McClelland and Kawamoto, additional concepts are defined corresponding to each of the micro-features they assigned. Here the male/female/neuter categorization of nouns and the doer/non-doer categorization of verbs is illustrated. McClelland and Kawamoto use eight dimensions along which nouns are categorized, and seven dimensions for verbs. Since the generation rules do not consider these features, this is not strictly necessary for "correct" rule abiding performance. It may enhance prototype effects, however.

```
;;;Rules that hold for all sentences
(DEFCONCEPT Sentence)
(ASSERT-CONCEPT 100 Sentence
  (RVM Has-Syntactic-Constituent Has-Semantic-Constituent))
(ASSERT-CONCEPT 100 Sentence
  (AND
    (SOME Has-Verb)
    (SOME Has-Subject-NP)))
(ASSERT-CONCEPT 100 (SOME Has-With-NP) (SOME Has-Object-NP))

;;;The generator "The <HUMAN> hit the <THING>."
(DEFCONCEPT HitAVP-Sentence
  (AND
    (FILLS Has-Verb Hit)
    (ALL Has-Subject-NP Human)
    (SOME Has-Object-NP)
    (DISJOINT (SOME Has-With-NP))))
(ASSERT-CONCEPT 100 HitAVP-Sentence
  (AND
    (RVM Has-Subject-NP Has-Agent)
    (RVM Has-Object-NP Has-Patient)
    (ALL Has-Verb Touch-Agent)))
```

Figure 8.5: The assertions that express the general task constraints and (one example of) the sentence generation rules. The concept HITAVP recognizes inputs generated by the hitAVP rule, and the associated assertions make sure the correct output results. Touch-Agent is one of the micro-features along the TOUCH dimension in which the Agent touches the patient. The (ALL Has-Verb Touch-Agent) assertion disambiguates "hit," which also has senses in which the agent does not touch the patient.

131

clauses disambiguate the nouns and verbs. An alternative is to ask what role a given noun fills, rather than asking what noun fills a given role. For example (WITH (ROLE ?) (FILLERS Man) (VR ?)).

8.4.3 Discussion

The one-for-one mapping of the nineteen rules onto concepts can be improved by defining a hierarchy of rule concepts each expressing sub-regularities. For instance, there is a regularity that if the Subject-NP is a HUMAN, then it is always assigned the role Agent.

Another correctable problem with the implementation in the figures is the proliferation of individuals. While McClelland and Kawamoto represent nouns using distributed patterns over 25 micro-features, μKLONE would use a local encoding over 26 individual nouns, 4 verbs, and one generic individual, which is always mapped to the current sentence. Since the ability to represent multiple role fillers is not needed, all the individuals standing for specific words can be eliminated. Instead, generic individuals can be recruited to stand for the words that occur in the current sentence, while the micro-features are input with VRs. The new version of the query for the sentence "The man hit the woman" is:

```
(QUERY
    '((WITH (ROLE Has-Subject-NP) (MIN 1) (VR (AND Human Male Large)))
     (WITH (ROLE Has-Verb) (MIN 1) (VR (AND Doer High-Intensity)))
     (WITH (ROLE Has-Object-NP) (MIN 1) (AND Human Female Large))
     (WITH (ROLE Has-Agent) (VR ?))
     (WITH (ROLE Has-Patient) (VR ?))
     (WITH (ROLE Has-Instrument) (VR ?))
     (WITH (ROLE Has-Modifier) (VR ?))
     (WITH (ROLE Has-Verb) (VR ?))))
```

An important question is whether a μKLONE implementation, based on a symbolic definition of the sentence generation rules, would exhibit the advantages McClelland and Kawamoto achieve by learning based on statistical regularities. Their primary goal

132

was to demonstrate simultaneous consideration of syntactic and semantic constraints in interpreting the sentences. Since both types of constraints are expressed as weighted assertions to be simultaneously satisfied, the μKLONE implementation shares this characteristic. The weights can be adjusted so that in some rules the syntactic constraint is more important, while in others semantic constraints dominate.

A μKLONE implementation would behave similarly with respect to ambiguity of lexical items and context-dependency of meanings. The word "bat" is categorized along known dimensions like NON-HUMAN rather strongly, and along ambiguous dimensions like SOFT either weakly (to express *a priori* probabilities) or not at all. Since {SOFT HARD} partitions NOUN, any instance of "bat" in a sentence will be filled out with a definite value along this dimension. McClelland and Kawamoto also discuss blending of patterns in certain sentences. If "The ball broke the window," ball takes on a higher value for the HARD micro-feature, because this is characteristic of BREAKERS. μKLONE can also override initial expectations based on context, although it's final answers lack any fuzziness with respect to any particular micro-feature. Still, the blending of interpretations at intermediate stages of the search has important effects, as discussed in the section on prototypes.

A more satisfying treatment of ambiguity would explicitly distinguish lexical items from meanings. Thus "bat" would be the Subject-NP, and BASEBALL-BAT would be the corresponding Instrument. However, the rules are now expressed using RVMs, which can only constrain the fillers of different roles to be the same individuals. If μKLONE had structural descriptions, the constraint could be expressed "In hitAVM sentences, the filler of the Agent role must be one of the meanings of the filler of the Subject-NP role."

A final implementation irk is the fact that sentences are described as flat structures in the μKLONE implementation. One would like to talk about "the object of the preposition in the prepositional phrase of the sentence" rather that "the With-NP." Lacking role-chains, however, the necessary constraints can only be expressed by flattening the description.

Of more significance is the lack of notions of time or causality. These play an important role not only in language understanding, but especially in planning. Lakoff suggests that people reason about such abstract concepts via metaphorical mappings onto spatial reasoning tasks, rather than propositional ones. Terry Regier [1988] has begun experiments on this kind of reasoning in connectionist networks. Following Lakoff, I believe that an entirely propositional KR system like μKLONE must be augmented with reasoners using different kinds of representation. I hope that the basic strategy of model-based reasoning using soft constraints will carry over.

9 Conclusion

9.1 Provides A Unifying Framework

μKLONE neatly combines Johnson-Laird's ideas about model-based reasoning, Levesque's ideas about vivid representations, and Hinton's ideas about distributed representations, none of which have been implemented in anything but a rudimentary way. Whereas connectionists have generally thought of their systems as diametrically opposed to logic-based systems, I have argued that the difference is not whether a formal logical semantics can be usefully applied, but whether the system uses sequential syntactic inference in which only information contained in a single rule is considered at one time, or parallel model-based inference in which all information simultaneously constrains the search.

Connectionist architectures provide the foundation for this unifying framework. They seem ideally suited for approximating probabilistic reasoning in complex domains. Using probability theory for describing mundane domains rather than defaults offers a concise way to ameliorate the anomalous extension problem. By defining a family of probability distributions from weighted assertions via the Boltzmann Distribution, and considering the zero temperature limit, the μKLONE semantics specifies a set of models provably contained in the set resulting from applying Reiter's default logic to the same (unweighted) assertions. This provides a way to relate probability theory and default logic.

Connectionist architectures have the drawback that the meaning of a unit is essentially fixed by the architecture, so it is difficult to have variables without simulating a higher-level machine. But model-based reasoning does not require variables. Given the particular non-logical constants of a theory, the space of possible models is well defined, and for finitely controllable languages only a finite subspace needs to be searched.

Connectionist systems using simulated annealing have the drawback that only one model is found, even when others may be equally good. But this is what Levesque suggests on more general grounds. Having a model allows the system to reason about the truth of each assertion independently, which is much simpler than detecting the inconsistency of arbitrary subsets of assertions. The notion of similarity between models arises directly out of the architecture, and the system naturally finds reasonable approximate answers. Finally, in model-based reasoning there is no place for abstractions like PROFESSIONAL-SAILOR, but only for primitive predicates. This is the essence of distributed representations, where these abstractions are strictly emergent properties of the unit-level representation. No inheritance algorithm is required to find the properties of a term, because they are explicit in the term's representation. No previous connectionist system has had a principled way to find appropriate primitives from which abstract concepts would emerge, nor performed any kind of emergent inheritance among roles.

9.2   Sequential Reasoning

In spite of the power to combine sources of evidence and to find plausible interpretations of incomplete and inconsistent information, there are hard limits to what a system like this can do. In many ways its reasoning is like perceptual reasoning, being fast, non-decomposable, inflexible, and only useful after lots of training (or tuning) in familiar situations. An intelligent agent must respond in unfamiliar situations as well. Since by definition these situations are unpredictable, it seems to require symbols with arbitrary referents. It is also impossible to predict the logical relations among individuals in a novel situation, so an analog parallel architecture will not in general be available. Even in familiar domains a problem involving causal chains like the full adder problem cannot be solved in parallel when the architecture is limited to representing only one frame at a time. It seems that sequential reasoning will be required, and concomitantly control structures and interpreters.

A hybrid production system in which the match is done by a connectionist KR module seems like a natural way to get both common sense behavior and sequential control. In such a system, the inner loop would be much more powerful than in current production systems, and many familiar problems could be solved in one match step. In other situations that require sequential reasoning and introspection, the full mundane KB would still play a part.

9.3   New Energy Functions

The Hopfield and Tank search method, in which units take on continuous values, is effective because the depth of an energy minimum is often reflected in the steepness of the gradient in that direction at the center of the search space. This is especially true in many of the classic connectionist testbed problems such as the traveling salesman problem, where the architecture is highly regular. The "structural constraints" do not favor any one solution over another, so the difference in the gradient in the direction of alternative syntactically correct solutions generally reflects differences in the data.

μKLONE's architecture is quite irregular, however. First, the fan-out of units in the Subject and Subject-Type groups is much higher than in the other two groups. Second, the KB language has many different constructs, and each one gives rise to a different constraint structure. An energy function that sums pairwise products of unit states is not very effective with this architecture. Not only are many extra units required to correctly implement the semantics, but also the structural constraints so skew the energy surface towards certain models, independent of the data, that the Hopfield and Tank method was not successful. The Boltzmann Machine simulated annealing search can be run slowly enough to guarantee correct performance, and indeed it did somewhat better than Hopfield and Tank on some early versions of μKLONE. But rectifying the problems with the energy function to make it smoother and to make the center of the search space an attractor of the structural constraints (see section 3.7.1) has worked much better. The special purpose energy functions do not fit the brain-like model of pairwise connections; hence it may be less misleading to call μKLONE a parallel constraint satisfaction system and not label it "connectionist." In this broader context, the approach of classifying constraints into the two categories "structural" and "domain," and then ensuring that the derivative of the former is zero in the center of the space appears promising. For different problems, the particular functions required may be different. IMPLIES is just one example, which proved to be useful in a logic-like domain.

9.4 Prospects for Practical Application

The expressive power of μKLONE's KB language seems adequate for some real-world applications. KL-ONE-style KR systems are being widely used, and the features that μKLONE lacks do not seem to be critical. The adequacy of the query language, and its semantics based on possibility rather than validity, is less certain, as are the effects of considering only information directly connected to the subject. In database applications, these restrictions pose no problem. Database queries normally relate only to a single subject, and there is little interaction between facts in the KB. A modified version of μKLONE, called CRUCS [Brachman and McGuinness, 1988], has been used as a database system using a domain twice as large as the Ted Turner domain. CRUCS is primarily designed to fill in the SUBJECT clause of queries, and it is able to retrieve the best-fitting individual on the first query, followed by successively poorer matches for each additional query.

The most spectacular possibility for application of μKLONE is as a learning expert system. Present successful expert systems incorporate KBs that are painstakingly constructed by hand. There are proposals for connectionist expert systems that would learn automatically, but it is difficult to give them initial domain-specific knowledge (Gallant [1987] is an exception). With μKLONE, experts could program an initial KB using a high level language, followed by automatic learning using the Boltzmann learning algorithm [Hinton and Sejnowski, 1986]. The hard part of automatic learning, forming the right concepts, would already be done. The system could do the fine tuning that seems harder for humans. Such a system would be ideal for domains like oil well-log interpretation, in which the relevant parameters are known, but a good set of rules is elusive.

The outlook for learning is uncertain. The network created from the Ted Turner KB is larger than any in which successful learning has been carried out before. Having several scales of constraint strengths is sure to be a problem, because it makes equilibrium distributions much harder to estimate. On the other hand, if learning is restricted to fine tuning the assertion strengths and the relation between the strengths of the five types of constraints, there are far fewer parameters to adjust than in other connectionist

138

networks.

Using a connectionist architecture to support approximate, model-based mundane reasoning is a promising technique. There are a number of variations on μKLONE's architecture that optimize its behavior for certain applications, such as DUCS and CRUCS, which are just beginning to be explored. Even if none of these architectures are successful, μKLONE has provided a new way to view the relationship between logic, probability, and connectionist networks.

A   Constraints

This appendix proves that any μKLONE constraint assigns an energy of zero to a model if the corresponding logical proposition is true in the model, and assigns it an energy greater than zero otherwise. This appendix treats the logically redundant, but pragmatically useful, constraints introduced in section 3.7.1 as well as the basic ones described in section 2.6. In translating a constraint into a proposition, the constraint types WITH-WEIGHT and VERY are ignored, and the differences between (IMPLIES p q) and (OR (NOT p) q) disappear. Therefore the mapping is many to one, and onto. Section 6.3 describes how these constraints are combined to implement μKLONE. The proofs proceed by induction on the complexity of the constraint.

> **Lemma:** <0-1-constraint>'s assign an energy of zero to models consistent with the constraint, and an energy in $< 0, 1]$ to other models.

Proof:

Base case: The constraint is an atomic proposition, TRUE, or FALSE. The table in figure A.2 shows the lemma to hold in this case.

Induction step: Assume that the arguments to any of the other <0-1-constraint>'s in the constraint grammar (figure A.1) satisfy the lemma. Then the energy function given in the table will also satisfy the lemma.

> **Theorem:** Any μKLONE constraint assigns an energy of zero to a model if the corresponding logical proposition is true in the model, and assigns it an energy greater than zero otherwise.

Proof:

```
<0-1-constraint>   ::=   TRUE
                    |    FALSE
                    |    <atomic-proposition>
                    |    (NOT <0-1-constraint>)
                    |    (OR <0-1-constraint>*)
                    |    (IMPLIES <constraint> <0-1-constraint>)
                    |    (EQUIV <0-1-constraint> <0-1-constraint>)
                    |    (MAX <0-1-constraint>*)
                    |    (PRETTY <0-1-constraint>)
                    |    (VERY <0-1-constraint>)
<constraint>       ::=   <0-1-constraint>
                    |    (AND <constraint>*)
                    |    (WITH-WEIGHT <positive-number> <constraint>)
                    |    (ATLEAST <whole-number> <0-1-constraint>*)
                    |    (ATMOST <whole-number> <0-1-constraint>*)
                    |    (EXACTLY <whole-number> <0-1-constraint>*)
```

Figure A.1: The constraint grammar. <0-1-constraint> is a subset of constraint types that assign every model an energy between zero and one.

Constraint	$E^m_{constraint}$	Purpose
p (atomic)	$\begin{cases} 0 \text{ if } p \text{ is true in } m \\ 1 \text{ otherwise} \end{cases}$	
(NOT p)	$1 - E^m_p$	Basic
(OR $p_1\ p_2\ \cdots\ p_n$)	$\lim\limits_{p \to -\infty} \left(\dfrac{1}{n} \sum\limits_{i=1}^{n} (E^m_{p_i})^p \right)^{\frac{1}{p}}$	translations
(AND $p_1\ p_2\ \cdots\ p_n$)	$\sum\limits_{i=1}^{n} E^m_{p_i}$	
(IMPLIES $p\ q$)	$\max(0, E^m_q - E^m_p)^k,\ k > 1$	Results in flatter energy surface than $\neg p \vee q$
(EQUIV $p\ q$)	$|E^m_p - E^m_q|^k,\ k > 1$	More efficient than $p \to q \wedge q \to p$
(MAX $p_1\ p_2\ \cdots\ p_n$)	$\lim\limits_{p \to \infty} \left(\dfrac{1}{n} \sum\limits_{i=1}^{n} (E^m_{p_i})^p \right)^{\frac{1}{p}}$	Substitutes for AND when energy range must be zero to one
(PRETTY p)	$(E^m_p)^k,\ k > 1$	True unless argument is very nearly false
(VERY p) $\equiv$ (NOT (PRETTY (NOT p)))		False unless argument is very nearly true
(WITH-WEIGHT $w\ p$)	$w \cdot E^m_p,\ w > 0$	Changes importance of component constraint
FALSE	1	Of little use,
TRUE	0	except in proofs
(ATLEAST $n\ p_1 \cdots p_k$) $\equiv$ (IMPLIES (AND (NOT p_1) $\cdots$ (NOT p_k)) (WITH-WEIGHT n FALSE))		
(ATMOST $n\ p_1 \cdots p_k$) $\equiv$ (IMPLIES (WITH-WEIGHT n FALSE) (AND (NOT p_1) $\cdots$ (NOT p_k)))		
(EXACTLY $n\ p_1 \cdots p_k$) $\equiv$ (EQUIV (AND (NOT p_1) $\cdots$ (NOT p_k)) (WITH-WEIGHT n FALSE))		

Figure A.2: A description of each constraint type, and its energy function.

Base case: The axiom is a <0-1-constraint>. By the lemma above, the energy assigned to a model is zero for models consistent with the constraint, and is greater than zero otherwise.

Induction step: Assume that the arguments to any of the other <constraint>'s in the constraint grammar satisfy the theorem. Then the energy function given in the table will also satisfy the theorem.

B   Complexity

This appendix provides a more rigorous argument than is given in section 4.4 that for consistent KBs μKLONE is equivalent in expressive power to the following decidable subset of first-order logic, which I will call the μKLONE class:

There is no equality predicate, and no function symbols except for constants. Predicates must have one or two arguments. Every time a variable appears as the second argument of a predicate it must appear with the same first argument. If that first argument is a variable, it must be the immediately governing one.

x governs y if the scope of the quantifier binding x properly includes that of the quantifier binding y [Dreben and Goldfarb, 1979]. x immediately governs y if there are no intermediate variables governed by x and governing y.

The equivalence is shown first, by a procedure for translating in either direction. Second, decidability is shown as a corollary of the stronger condition of finite controllability; for any μKLONE theory, it is possible to compute a bound, Ω, such that if the theory has a model, it has a model with no more than Ω individuals. In principle all of these possible models can be checked against the theory.

A lower bound on the complexity of query answering is provided by comparison with $\mathcal{FL}$, a language in which answering subsumption questions is co-NP hard [Brachman and Levesque, 1984]. Its syntax is:

Sentences with μKLONE equivalent	Sentences without μKLONE equivalent
$\forall xy\, Pxy$	$\forall xy\, (Pxy \lor Pyx)$
$\exists x\, Pxc \land Pxd$	$\exists x\, Pcx \land Pdx$
$\forall x \exists y \forall z\, Pxy \lor Qyz$	$\forall x \exists y \forall z\, Pxy \lor Qyz \lor Rxz$
$Pcd \lor Pdc$	$\exists x\, Pxx$

Figure B.1: Examples of sentences contained in the above subset of FOL, and examples that aren't. c and d are constants.

```
<concept> ::= <atom>
              — (AND <concept>*)
              — (ALL <role> <concept>)
              — (SOME <role>)
<role>    ::= <atom>
              — (RESTR <role> <concept>)
```

This language becomes a subset of μKLONE when the construct (RESTR <role> <concept>) is translated as (AND <role> (RANGE <concept>)). The subsumption question (subsumesp C1 C2) is true if and only if (query '((SUBJECT-TYPE (AND C2 (DISJOINT C1))))) is unsatisfiable. Similarly for roles, to find if (subsumesp R1 R2) one asks (query '((WITH (ROLE (AND R2 (DISJOINT R1))) (MINIMUM-FILLERS 1)))).

A co-NP hard problem has been reduced to the complement of query answering, which must therefore be NP-hard.

The decision problem asks simply whether a theory has a model. μKLONE's goal is rather to find a "best" interpretation, and so the analysis in this appendix does not reveal all that one would like to know about its competence. It is unknown whether there is an algorithm guaranteed to terminate in finite time that will find a best interpretation of queries in the case where the union of the KB and the presuppositions of the query is inconsistent.

Since the decision problem is a binary one, the numerical value of the certainties attached to the assertions are unimportant, and are here assumed to be 1.

B.1 μKLONE to Logic

This section shows that the logical translation of any μKLONE KB is in fact in the μKLONE class. The proof proceeds by structural induction. Each rewrite rule in the μKLONE grammar is shown to preserve the restrictions.

The KB is assumed to consist only of assertions, the definition macros having been already expanded. Similarly, OR, RVM, and the two-argument SOME have been eliminated.

144

Certainties are ignored.

There are countably many atomic concepts (one-place predicate symbols) $c_1, \ldots, c_n$, atomic roles (two-place predicate symbols) $r_1, \ldots, r_n$, and individual constants $i_1, \ldots, i_n$.

Assertion-forming rules:

ASSERT-CONCEPT If C_1 and C_2 are concepts, and x is a variable foreign to C_1 and C_2, then $\forall x(C_1 x \rightarrow C_2 x)$ is an assertion.

ASSERT-ROLE If R_1 and R_2 are roles, and x and y are variables foreign to R_1 and R_2, then $\forall xy(R_1 xy \rightarrow R_2 xy)$ is an assertion.

INSTANTIATE-CONCEPT If C is a concept, and i is an individual constant, then Ci is an assertion.

INSTANTIATE-ROLE If R is a role, and i_1 and i_2 are individual constants, then $Ri_1 i_2$ is an assertion.

Concept-forming rules:

SOME If R is a role, and x and z are variables foreign to R, then $\lambda x \exists z R x z$ is a concept.

ALL If R is a role, C is a concept, and x and z are variables foreign to R and C, then $\lambda x \forall z(Rxz \rightarrow Cz)$ is a concept.

DISJOINT If C is a concept, then $\neg C$ is a concept.

AND If $C_1, \ldots, C_n$ are concepts, then $(\wedge \, C_1, \ldots, C_n)$ is a concept.

FILLS If R is a role, i is an individual constant, and x is a variable foreign to R, then $\lambda x R x i$ is a concept.

Role-forming rules:

DISJOINT If R is role, then $\neg R$ is a role.

AND If $R_1, \ldots, R_n$ are roles, then $(\wedge \, R_1, \ldots, R_n)$ is a role.

DOMAIN If C is a concept, and x and y are variables foreign to C, then $\lambda xy C x$ is a role.

145

RANGE If C is a concept, and x and y are variables foreign to C, then $\lambda xyCy$ is a role.

Clearly, there is no equality predicate, no function symbols other than constants, nor predicates with other than one or two arguments. Variables appear as the second argument to predicates in the rules for ASSERT-ROLE, SOME, and ALL. In each case it is a new variable, appearing with a first argument that is the immediately governing variable, or a lambda variable. The lambda conversion can happen as a result of applying the rule for ASSERT-CONCEPT, INSTANTIATE-CONCEPT, ALL, DOMAIN, or RANGE. In the first case, the lambda variable is converted to the immediately governing variable; in the second it is converted to a constant. In the last two cases an additional lambda variable is added to the expression. Upon eventual lambda conversion, the extra variable, which is not used, can be eliminated, and these two cases reduce to the previous ones.

B.2 Logic to μKLONE

This section translates in the other direction, showing that any sentence in the μKLONE class has an equivalent μKLONE KB. Again, the proof is by structural induction, with one rule for every rewrite rule in the grammar for the subset of logic.

To use the proof constructively to find the translation of a formula, $\forall x$ must everywhere be replaced by $\neg\exists x\neg$. Variables should be renamed so that no two quantifiers introduce variables with the same name. Also, quantifiers must be pushed in a far as possible.

There are countably many one-place predicate symbols $c_1,\ldots,c_n$, two-place predicate symbols $r_1,\ldots,r_n$, and individual constants $i_1,\ldots,i_n$.

Convert roleform to KB If F is a roleform, then ((ASSERT-ROLE (AND) F)) is a KB.

(AND) is vacuously true, so this asserts that the two-place predicate F is true for all pairs of arguments. In this proof, all subformulas are forced into the roleform mold, which accounts for the appearance of some silly predicates, like $\lambda xy\ Ci$.

146

One-place predication of a variable If C is a one-place predicate symbol, then (RANGE C) is a roleform.

One-place predication of a constant If C is a one-place predicate symbol and i is an individual constant, then (RANGE (FILLS (RANGE C) i)) is a roleform.

Justification: (RANGE (FILLS (RANGE C) i)) translates to $\lambda uv(\lambda x(\lambda yz Cz)(xi))(v) = \lambda uv\ Ci$.

Two-place predication, second argument is a variable (whether first argument is a constant or a variable depends on which EXISTS form is used to introduce the variable) If R is a two-place predicate symbol, then R is a roleform.

Two-place predication of a variable and a constant If R is a two-place predicate symbol, and i is an individual constant, then (RANGE (FILLS R i)) is a roleform.

Justification: (RANGE (FILLS R i)) translates to $\lambda uv(\lambda x\ Rxi)(v) = \lambda uv\ Rvi$.

Two-place predication of constants If R is a two-place predicate symbol, and i_1 and i_2 are individual constants, then (RANGE (FILLS (RANGE (FILLS R i_2)) i_1)) is a roleform.

Justification: (RANGE (FILLS (RANGE (FILLS R i_2)) i_1)) translates to $\lambda mn(\lambda u(\lambda xy(\lambda z\ Rzi_2)(y))(ui_1))(n) = \lambda mn\ Ri_1 i_2$.

AND If $F_1, \ldots, F_n$ are roleforms, then (AND $F_1, \ldots, F_n$) is a roleform.

OR If $F_1, \ldots, F_n$ are roleforms, then (OR $F_1, \ldots, F_n$) is a roleform.

NOT If F is a roleform, then (DISJOINT F) is a roleform.

EXISTS x, x appears after the constant i If F is a roleform and i is an individual constant, then (RANGE (FILLS (RANGE (SOME F)) i)) is a roleform.

Justification: (RANGE (FILLS (RANGE (SOME F)) i)) translates to $\lambda mn(\lambda r(\lambda uv(\lambda x\exists z\ Fxz)(v))(ri))(n) = \lambda mn\ \exists z\ Fiz$.

EXISTS x, x doesn't appear after a constant If F is a roleform, then (RANGE (SOME F)) is a roleform.

Justification: (RANGE (SOME F)) translates to $\lambda uv(\lambda x \exists z\ Fxz)(v) = \lambda uv \exists z\ Fvz$.

Clearly, *every* sentence in FOL can be translated using these rules. This question is, do those sentences meeting the restrictions get translated correctly. The structural correspondence directly follows from the rules: The logical connectives are translated as equivalent μKLONE constructs; existentials are translated into an ugly μKLONE expression, which on translation back into logic and lambda reduction gives back an existential; and the translation rules for predication also produce μKLONE constructs that reverse translate back to lambda expressions containing the original form. Ensuring that the correct skeletal structure results is not enough, however. Since the variables, which are explicit in the FOL representation, are implicit in the μKLONE representation, we must ensure that they are correctly matched up with the quantifiers. The key is the assumption made above, that all quantifiers are pushed in as far as possible. For one-place predicates, this means the innermost quantifier in whose scope the predicate appears is the one introducing the variable that is the argument of the predicate. For two-place predicates whose arguments are both variables one must immediately govern the other, and they must therefore be introduced by the two innermost quantifiers. The restriction that a variable always appear with the same first argument is a reflection of the variables being implicit, and thus having to reflect the quantifier nesting.

B.3 The Decidability of Query Answering

The subset of FOL expressible in μKLONE, minus constants, is contained in the finitely controllable class 6.2 of Dreben and Goldfarb. Allowing constants in the language does not affect the finite controllability. Dreben and Goldfarb mention a "vivid subclass" of class 6.2:

> The class of all prenex schemata $Q_1 v_1 \cdots Q_p v_p F^M$ whose bases contain, aside from one-membered sets, just each set $\{v_i, v_{i+1}\}, 1 \leq i \leq p$.

The bases of a formula are the sets of variables that appear together as arguments of a predicate symbol. Thus one-place predicates, and two-place predicates one of whose

148

arguments is constant, give rise to one-membered sets. Because the first argument to two-place predicates, when both arguments are variables, must immediately govern the second, the requirement about the bases of the vivid subclass is met. However not all sentences in the μKLONE class can be put in prenex form without violating these requirements. For instance, prenexing the sentence $\forall x[(\forall y\, Pxy) \lor (\forall z\, Qxz)]$ will destroy the immediate-governing relation between the arguments to one of the atoms.

However, using the Splitting Lemma of Dreben and Goldfarb, it is always possible to find a sentence in the vivid subclass that is satisfiable over the same universe. With the Splitting Lemma, nested subformulas can be split off and unnested.

> **Splitting Lemma.** Let F be a formula and let G be a subformula of F that occurs only positively in F and that contains only one free variable v (G may contain quantifiers). Let P be a monadic predicate letter foreign to F; let F_1 be the result of substituting Pv for G in F, and let F_2 be $\forall v(Pv \to G)$. Then F and $F_1 \land F_2$ are satisfiable over the same universe.

The proof below was supplied by Warren Goldfarb (personal communication):

Let F be a formula in the μKLONE class; we may assume that negation signs are pushed in, so that no quantifier lies in the scope of a negation sign. Let $(Qy)H$ be a subformula of F, where y is immediately governed by a variable v and H is quantifier-free (thus (Qy) is an innermost quantifier). Each atomic subformula of H either (a) does not contain y or (b) contains y as its only variable or (c) contains just y and v.

Suppose first that Q is $\forall$. By truth-functional logic, we may take H to have the form $(A_1 \lor B_1) \land (A_2 \lor B_2) \land \cdots \land (A_k \lor B_k)$, where each A_i is a disjunction of signed atomic subformulas of type (a) and each B_i is a disjunction of signed atomic subformulas of types (b) and (c). Then $(\forall y)H$ is equivalent to $(A_1 \lor (\forall y)B_1) \land (A_2 \lor (\forall y)B_2) \land \cdots \land (A_k \lor (\forall y)B_k)$. Now let $P_1, P_2, \ldots, P_k$ be monadic predicate letters foreign to F, and let F' be the formula obtained from F by replacing the subformula $(\forall y)H$ with the formula $(A_1 \lor P_1 v) \land (A_2 \lor P_2 v) \land \cdots \land (A_k \lor P_k v)$. Let F'' be the conjunction $(\forall v)[(P_1 v \to (\forall y)B_1) \land (P_2 v \to (\forall y)B_2) \land \cdots \land (P_k v \to (\forall y)B_k)]$. Then by the Splitting Lemma, F is satisfiable over the same universe as $F' \land F''$. F'' is purely universal, and F' is in the μKLONE class but has less quantifier-nesting than the original formula F.

149

If Q is $\exists$, a similar procedure works, except that the truth-functional step puts H in the form $(A_1 \wedge B_1) \vee \cdots \vee (A_k \wedge B_k)$, so that $(\exists y)H$ is equivalent to $(A_1 \wedge (\exists y)B_1) \vee \cdots \vee (A_k \wedge (\exists y)B_k)$; and the conjuncts of F'' are $(P_i v \rightarrow (\exists y)B_i)$. In this case, F'' is $\forall(\exists \wedge \cdots \wedge \exists)$ (rather than purely universal); F', as before, has less quantifier-nesting than F.

The procedure can be repeated. Eventually we obtain a formula $F^* \wedge F_1 \wedge \cdots \wedge F_m$, where F^* has only one quantifier, and each F_i is either purely universal or $\forall(\exists \wedge \cdots \wedge \exists)$. By prenexing in left-to-right order, the requirements of the vivid subclass are met.

It is also possible to calculate a bound, Ω, such that if a formula in class 6.2 has a model, it has a model with no more than Ω individuals. This calculation is not very illuminating, but is given here nevertheless. A y-variable is a variable that is introduced by a universal quantifier preceded by an even number of negation signs, or by an existential quantifier preceded by an odd number of negation signs. Other variables are x-variables. A Herbrand instance of order r of a formula is a variable-free formula in which the x-variables are replaced by Skolem functions and the y-variables are replaced by elements of the domain of the formula of order r. The domain of a formula of order r is the set of variable-free terms generated from a constant a and the Skolem functions, where the maximum nesting depth of function application is p. A formula has a model if and only if it satisfies all its Herbrand instances of some order.

The finite controllability of class 6.2 is shown by reduction to class 6.1, which in turn can be reduced to class 2.7. For class 2.7, a formula has a model if and only if it satisfies all its Herbrand instances of order $m! \cdot 2^{p \cdot m^l}$, where p is the number of predicate letters in the formula, l is the maximum number of argument places of these letters (2 for μKLONE), and m is the number of y-variables. In μKLONE both p and m are bounded by the size of the KB, n. The size of the domain of a formula, F, of order r, $d(F,r)$, is $d(F,r-1)$ plus, for each Skolem function of q arguments, the number of ways to choose q arguments from $d(F,r-1)$ elements with replacement, $d(F,r-1)^q$. q is also bounded by the KB size. Therefore, $d(F,r) \leq 2^{2(q+1)^{r-1}}$. Overall, the number of individuals required is bounded by $\Omega \leq 2^{2(n+1)^{n! \cdot 2^{n^3}}}$ where n is the size of the KB.

150

C Notation

Item	Examples
Concept	PERSON (ALL HAS-JOB ARMCHAIR-ACTIVITY)
Role	HAS-JOB
Individual	Corporate-Raiding
μKLONE Language Fragment	(ASSERT-CONCEPT 100 Person Animal) WITH
Constraint	IMPLIES
Group	Role-Filler-Types Group
Proposition	*has-hobby(Ted, Sailing)* *(All has-job armchair-activity)(Ted)*
Unit	*has-hobby(subject, Sailing)* *subject=Sailing* *<Unit 0 of Subject-Type-IO-1 Group>*

D Syntax

<query>   ::=   ({(SUBJECT <i>)} (SUBJECT-TYPE <c>)* <with form>*)
<with form> ::=   (WITH {(ROLE <r>)} {(VR <c>)}
                            {(FILLERS <i-list>)} {(MINIMUM-FILLERS <n>)})
<c>   ::=   <concept> | ?
<r>   ::=   <role> | ?
<i>   ::=   <individual> | ?
<n>   ::=   <whole number> | ?
<i-list>   ::=   <i> | (<individual>*)

Figure D.1: Query Language Syntax. Query arguments and arguments to WITH forms may appear in any order. The number of SUBJECT-TYPE and WITH forms is limited by the implementation; four or five seems sufficient.

```
       <KB>  ::=  (<S>*)
        <S>  ::=  (DEFCONCEPT <concept> (PRIMITIVE))
              |   (DEFCONCEPT <concept> <concept form>)
              |   (ASSERT-CONCEPT
                      <certainty> <concept form> <concept form>)
              |   (DEFROLE <role> (PRIMITIVE))
              |   (DEFROLE <role> <role form>)
              |   (ASSERT-ROLE <certainty> <role form> <role form>)
              |   (INSTANTIATE-CONCEPT
                      <certainty> <concept form> <individual>)
              |   (INSTANTIATE-ROLE
                      <certainty> <individual> <role form> <individual>)
<concept form>  ::=  <concept>
              |   (DISJOINT <concept form>)
              |   (AND <concept form>*)
              |   (OR <concept form>*)
              |   (ALL <role form> <concept form>)
              |   (SOME <role form>)
              |   (SOME <role form> <concept form>)
              |   (FILLS <role form> <individual>)
              |   (RVM <role form> <role form>)
   <role form>  ::=  <role>
              |   (DISJOINT <role form>)
              |   (AND <role form>*)
              |   (OR <role form>*)
              |   (DOMAIN <concept form>)
              |   (RANGE <concept form>)
     <concept>  ::=  <symbol>
        <role>  ::=  <symbol>
  <individual>  ::=  <symbol>
   <certainty>  ::=  <positive real number>
```

Figure D.2: KB Language Syntax. OR, RVM and the two-argument SOME do not add to the expressive power of the language. They are macros that are expanded into the remaining constructs. Having both ALL and SOME is redundant, too, but both are implemented directly.

E   Architecture

Group	Function
Subject Group	*Which individual is the subject.* *Copies type of that individual into Subject-Type Group,* *and role-fillers of that individual in Role-Fillers group.*
Subject-Type Group	*The subject's type.* *Imposes constraints on the Role-Fillers Group.*
Role-Fillers Group	*Represents each individual's relations to the subject.*
Role-Filler-Types Group	*Represents the type of every individual.*
Subject-Type-IO Groups	*If clamped, forces type information into Subject-Type Group.* *If not clamped, reads out the subject's type.*
Role-IO Groups	*Specifies the role that VR, FILLERS,* *and MINIMUM-FILLERS groups apply to.*
VR-IO Groups	*Imposes or reads out type restrictions on fillers.*
Fillers-IO Groups	*Specifies or reads out the fillers.*
MINIMUM-FILLERS-IO Groups	*Specifies or reads out the number of fillers.*

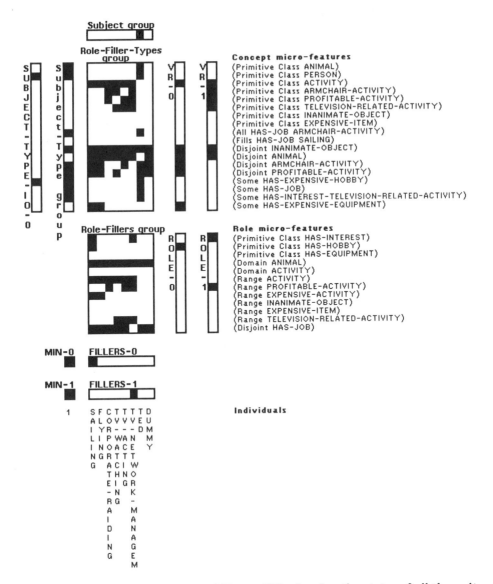

Figure E.1: Network built from the Ted Turner KB, showing the states of all the units at the end of an annealing search to answer the sample query discussed in the text. The Subject group was clamped to force Ted to be the subject of the query, and the Subject-Type group was clamped to force the subject to be a SELF-MADE-MILLIONAIRE-PLAYBOY. Role-0 was clamped to tell the MINIMUM-FILLERS-0, Fillers-0, and VR-0 groups to pay attention to the HAS-HOBBY role. Thus the pattern in MINIMUM-FILLERS-0 means there is at least one filler of the HAS-HOBBY role; the pattern in Fillers-0 means that Sailing is a filler of the HAS-HOBBY role; and the pattern in VR-0 means that all fillers of the HAS-HOBBY role are non-armchair, non-profitable, expensive activities. Similarly for the second set of IO groups, since HAS-JOB was clamped into Role-1, the pattern in MINIMUM-FILLERS-1 means Ted has at least one job; the pattern in Fillers-1 means TV-Network-Management is his job; and the pattern in VR-1 means that all his jobs are armchair, profitable, television-related activities.

References

[Abrett and Burstein, 1987] Glenn Abrett and Mark H. Burstein. The KREME knowl-edge editing environment. *International Journal of Man-Machine Studies*, 27:103–126, 1987. (Also in Proceedings of the Knowledge Acquisition for Knowledge-Based Systems Workshop, Banff, Canada, Nov. 1986.

[Ackley, 1987] David H. Ackley. *A connectionist machine for genetic hillclimbing.* Kluwer Academic Publishers, Boston, 1987. Also published as a 1987 CMU PhD thesis.

[Brachman and Levesque, 1984] Ronald J. Brachman and Hector J. Levesque. The tractability of subsumption in frame-based description languages. In *Proceedings of the Fourth National Conference on Artificial Intelligence*, pages 34–37, Austin, Texas, August 1984.

[Brachman and McGuinness, 1988] Ronald J. Brachman and Deborah L. McGuinness. Knowledge representation, connectionism, and conceptual retrieval. In *Proceedings of the 11th International Conference on Research and Development in Information Retrieval*, pages 161–174, 47X. 38040 Grenoble Cedex - France, June 1988. Presses UniPresses Universitaires de Grenoble.

[Brachman and Schmolze, 1985] Ronald J. Brachman and James G. Schmolze. An overview of the KL-ONE knowledge representation system. *Cognitive Science*, 9(2):171–216, March 1985.

[Brachman et al., 1983] Ronald J. Brachman, Richard E. Fikes, and Hector J. Levesque. Krypton: A functional approach to knowledge representation. *IEEE Computer*, 16(10):67–73, October 1983.

[Brachman et al., 1985] Ronald J. Brachman, Victoria P. Gilbert, and Hector J. Levesque. An essential hybrid reasoning system: Knowledge and symbol level accounts of Krypton. In *Proceedings of the Ninth International Joint Conference on Artificial Intelligence*, pages 532–539, Los Angeles, California, August 1985.

[Brachman, 1978] Ronald J. Brachman. A structural paradigm for representing knowl-edge. Technical Report 3605, Bolt Beranek and Newman Inc., May 1978. This is a revised version of a 1977 Harvard PhD Thesis.

[Brachman, 1979] Ronald J. Brachman. On the epistemological status of semantic networks. In Nicholas V. Findler, editor, *Associative Networks: Representation and Use of Knowledge by Computers*, pages 3–50. Academic Press, New York, 1979.

[Brachman, 1985] Ronald J. Brachman. 'I lied about the trees' (or, defaults and definitions in knowledge representation). *AI Magazine*, 6(3):80–93, 1985.

[Brown, 1958] Roger Brown. How shall a thing be called? *Psychological Review*, 65:14–21, 1958.

[Carnap, 1950] Rudolf Carnap. *Logical Foundations of Probability*, chapter 2, pages 19–51. University of Chicago Press, Chicago, 1950.

[Charniak, 1986] Eugene Charniak. A neat theory of marker passing. In *Proceedings of the Fifth National Conference on Artificial Intelligence*, pages 584–588, Philadelphia, Pennsylvania, August 1986.

[Chernoff and Moses, 1959] Herman Chernoff and Lincoln E. Moses. *Elementary Decision Theory*. Wiley, New York, 1959.

[de Kleer and Brown, 1984] Johan de Kleer and John Seely Brown. A qualitative physics based on confluences. *Artificial Intelligence*, 24:7–83, 1984.

[de Kleer, 1984] Johan de Kleer. Choices without backtracking. In *Proceedings of the Fourth National Conference on Artificial Intelligence*, pages 79–85, Austin, Texas, 1984.

[de Kleer, 1986] Johan de Kleer. An assumption-based TMS. *Artificial Intelligence*, 28:127–162, 1986.

[Denker *et al.*, 1987] John Denker, Daniel Schwartz, Ben Wittner, Sara Solla, John Hopfield, Richard Howard, and Lawrence Jackel. Automatic learning, rule extraction, and generalization. Technical report, AT&T Bell Laboratories and California Institute of Technology, 1987.

[Derthick and Tebelskis, 1988] Mark Derthick and Joe Tebelskis. 'Ensemble' Boltzmann units have collective computational properties like those of Hopfield and Tank neurons. In *Proceedings of the IEEE Conference on Neural Information Processing Systems*, pages 223–232. American Institute of Physics, 1988.

[Derthick, 1987] Mark Derthick. Counterfactual reasoning with direct models. In *Proceedings of the Sixth National Conference on Artificial Intelligence*, pages 346–351, Seattle, Washington, July 1987.

[Dolan and Dyer, 1988] Charles P. Dolan and Michael G. Dyer. Parallel retrieval and application of conceptual knowledge. In David S. Touretzky, Geoffrey E. Hinton, and Terrence J. Sejnowski, editors, *Proceedings of the 1988 Connectionist Models Summer School*. Morgan Kaufmann, 1988.

[Dolan, 1989] Charles P. Dolan. *Tensor Manipulation Networks: Connectionist and Symbolic Approaches to Comprehension, Learning, and Planning*. PhD thesis, UCLA, 1989. Available as Artificial Intelligence Laboratory Technical Report UCLA-AI-89-06.

[Dreben and Goldfarb, 1979] Burton Dreben and Warren D. Goldfarb. *The decision problem: solvable classes of quantificational formulas*. Addison-Wesley, Reading, Massachusetts, 1979.

[Duda *et al.*, 1979] Richard O. Duda, John Gaschnig, and Peter E. Hart. Model design in the prospector consultant system for mineral exploration. In Donald Michie, editor, *Expert Systems in the micro-electronic age*, pages 153–167. Edinburgh University Press, 1979.

[Fahlman, 1979] Scott E. Fahlman. *NETL: A system for representing and using real-world knowledge*. MIT Press, Cambridge, Mass., 1979.

[Feldman and Ballard, 1982] Jerome A. Feldman and Dana H. Ballard. Connectionist models and their properties. *Cognitive Science*, 6:205–254, 1982.

[Fillmore, 1968] Charles J. Fillmore. The case for case. In E. Bach and R. T. Harms, editors, *Universals in Linguistic Theory*, pages 1–88. Holt, Rinehart, and Winston, New York, 1968.

[Forbus, 1984] Kenneth Forbus. Qualitative process theory. *Artificial Intelligence*, 24:85–168, April 1984.

[Gallant, 1987] Steve I. Gallant. Connectionist expert systems. Unpublished manuscript, Northeastern University, July 1987.

[Garey and Johnson, 1979] Michael R. Garey and David S. Johnson. *Computers and intractability: a guide to the theory of NP-completeness*. W. H. Freeman, San Francisco, 1979.

[Geffner and Pearl, 1987] Hector Geffner and Judea Pearl. On the probabilistic semantics of connectionist networks. In Maureen Caudill and Charles Butler, editors, *Proceedings of the IEEE First International Conference of Neural Networks*, volume II, pages 187–195, June 1987.

[Geman and Geman, 1984] Stuart Geman and Donald Geman. Stochastic relaxation, Gibbs distributions, and the Bayesian restoration of images. *IEEE Transactions on Pattern Analysis and Machine Intelligence*, PAMI-6:721–741, 1984.

[Genesereth, 1984] M.R. Genesereth. The use of design descriptions in automated diagnosis. *Artificial Intelligence*, 24, 1984.

[Ginsberg, 1986] Matthew Ginsberg. Counterfactuals. *Artificial Intelligence*, 30:35–79, 1986.

[Haimowitz, 1988] Ira J. Haimowitz. Using NIKL in a large medical knowledge base. Technical Report MIT/LCS/TM-348, MIT, January 1988.

[Harrah, 1984] David Harrah. The logic of questions. In Dov Gabbay and Franz Guenthner, editors, *Handbook of Philosophical Logic*, volume II. D. Reidel, 1984.

[Henrion, 1986] M. Henrion. Propagating uncertainty by probabilistic logic sampling in Bayesian networks. In *Second AAAI Workshop in Artificial Intelligence*. AAAI, August 1986.

[Hinton and Sejnowski, 1983] Geoffrey E. Hinton and Terrence J. Sejnowski. Analyzing cooperative computation. In *Proceedings of the Fifth Annual Conference of the Cognitive Science Society*, Rochester, NY, May 1983. Cognitive Science Society.

[Hinton and Sejnowski, 1986] Geoffrey E. Hinton and Terrence J. Sejnowski. Learning and relearning in Boltzmann Machines. In David E. Rumelhart, James L. McClelland, and the PDP research group, editors, *Parallel distributed processing: Explorations in*

159

the microstructure of cognition. Volume I, chapter 7, pages 282–317. Bradford Books, Cambridge, MA, 1986.

[Hinton *et al.*, 1986] Geoffrey E. Hinton, James L. McClelland, and David E. Rumelhart. Distributed representations. In David E. Rumelhart, James L. McClelland, and the PDP research group, editors, *Parallel distributed processing: Explorations in the microstructure of cognition. Volume I*, chapter 3, pages 77–109. Bradford Books, Cambridge, MA, 1986.

[Hinton, 1977] Geoffrey E. Hinton. *Relaxation and its role in vision*. PhD thesis, University of Edinburgh, 1977. Described in: Ballard, D. H., & Brown, C. M, *Computer Vision*, Englewood Cliffs NJ: Printice-Hall, 1982, 408-430.

[Hinton, 1981] Geoffrey E. Hinton. Implementing semantic networks in parallel hardware. In Geoffrey E. Hinton and James A. Anderson, editors, *Parallel Models of Associative Memory*, chapter 6, pages 161–188. Erlbaum, Hillsdale, NJ, 1981.

[Hinton, 1986] Geoffrey E. Hinton. Learning distributed representations of concepts. In *Proceedings of the Eighth Annual Cognitive Science Conference*, pages 1–12, Amherst, Massachusetts, 1986. Cognitive Science Society.

[Hinton, 1988] Geoffrey E. Hinton. Representing part-whole hierarchies in connectionist networks. In *Proceedings of the Tenth Annual Conference of the Cognitive Science Society*, Montreal, Canada, August 1988.

[Hofstadter, 1985] Douglas R. Hofstadter. *Metamagical Themas*. Basic Books, New York, 1985.

[Holland, 1986] John Holland. Escaping brittleness: The possibilities of general-purpose learning algorithms applied to parallel rule-based systems. In Ryszard Michalski, Jaime Carbonell, and Tom Mitchell, editors, *Machine Learning, Volume 2*, chapter 20, pages 593–623. Morgan Kaufmann, 1986.

[Hopfield, 1984] John J. Hopfield. Neurons with graded response have collective computational properties like those of two-state neurons. *Proceedings of the National Academy of Sciences U.S.A.*, 81:3088–3092, May 1984.

[Horty and Thomason, 1987] John F. Horty and Richmond H. Thomason. Mixing strict and defeasible inheritance. In *Proceedings of the Seventh National Conference on Artificial Intelligence*, pages 427–43, Saint Paul, Minnesota, 1987.

[Horty *et al.*, 1987] John F. Horty, Richmond H. Thomason, and David S. Touretzky. A skeptical theory of inheritance in nonmonotonic semantic networks. In *Proceedings of the Sixth National Conference on Artificial Intelligence*, pages 358–363, Seattle, Washington, 1987.

[Horty, 1988] John Horty. A theory of defeasible argument. Unpublished manuscript, Carnegie-Mellon University, 1988.

[John and McClelland, 1988] Mark F. St. John and James L. McClelland. Learning and applying contextual constraints in sentence comprehension. Technical report, Carnegie-Mellon University, Department of Psychology, Pittsburgh, PA, 1988.

[Johnson-Laird, 1983] Philip N. Johnson-Laird. *Mental Models*. Harvard University Press, Cambridge, Massachusetts, 1983.

[Kirkpatrick *et al.*, 1983] S. Kirkpatrick, C. D. Gelatt, Jr., and M. P. Vecchi. Optimization by simulated annealing. *Science*, 220:671–680, 1983.

[Konolige, 1979] Kurt Konolige. Bayesian methods for updating probabilities. In *A Computer-Based Consultant for Mineral Exploration*, pages 83–146. SRI International, 1979.

[Lakoff, 1987] George Lakoff. *Women, Fire, and Dangerous Things: What Categories Reveal about the Mind*. University of Chicago Press, 1987.

[Levesque, 1986] Hector J. Levesque. Making believers out of computers. *Artificial Intelligence*, 30:81–108, 1986.

[Mac Gregor and Bates, 1987] Robert Mac Gregor and Raymond Bates. The Loom knowledge representation language. Technical Report ISI/RS-87-188, University of Southern California/Information Sciences Institute, May 1987.

[Mark, 1981] William Mark. Representation and inference in the consul system. In *Proceedings of the Seventh International Joint Conference on Artificial Intelligence*, pages 375–381, Vancouver, B. C., August 1981.

[Marroquin, 1985] Jose Luis Marroquin. *Probabilistic Solution of Inverse Problems*. PhD thesis, MIT, September 1985.

[McCarthy, 1968] John McCarthy. Programs with common sense. In Marvin L. Minsky, editor, *Semantic Information Processing*, chapter 7, pages 403–418. MIT Press, Cambridge, Massachusetts, 1968.

[McCarthy, 1977] John McCarthy. Epistemological problems in artificial intelligence. In *Proceedings of the Fifth International Joint Conference on Artificial Intelligence*, pages 1038–1044, 1977.

[McClelland and Kawamoto, 1986] James L. McClelland and Alan H. Kawamoto. Mechanisms of sentence processing: Assigning roles to constituents. In James L. McClelland, David E. Rumelhart, and the PDP research group, editors, *Parallel distributed processing: Explorations in the microstructure of cognition. Volume II*, chapter 19, pages 272–326. Bradford Books, Cambridge, MA, 1986.

[McClelland, 1981] James L. McClelland. Retrieving general and specific information from stored knowledge of specifics. In *Proceedings of the Third Annual Conference of the Cognitive Science Society*, pages 170–172, Berkeley, California, August 1981.

[Minsky and Papert, 1969] Marvin Minsky and Seymour Papert. *Perceptrons*. MIT Press, Cambridge, Mass, 1969.

[Minsky, 1975] Marvin L. Minsky. A framework for representing knowledge. In Patrick H. Winston, editor, *The Psychology of Computer Vision*, chapter 6, pages 211–277. McGraw Hill, New York, 1975.

[Morris, 1988] Paul H. Morris. The anomalous extension problem in default reasoning. *Artificial Intelligence*, 35:383–399, 1988.

[Nebel, 1988] Bernhard Nebel. Computational complexity of terminological reasoning in BACK. *Artificial Intelligence*, 34:371–383, 1988.

[Newell, 1982] Allen Newell. The knowledge level. *Artificial Intelligence*, 18(1):87–127, 1982.

[Patel-Schneider, 1984] Peter F. Patel-Schneider. Small can be beautiful in knowledge representation. In *IEEE Workshop on Principles of Knowledge-Based Systems*. IEEE,

1984.

[Patel-Schneider, 1987] Peter F. Patel-Schneider. *Decidable, Logic-Based Knowledge Representation*. PhD thesis, University of Toronto, May 1987.

[Patel-Schneider, 1988] Peter F. Patel-Schneider. Undecidability of subsumption in NIKL. Unpublished Manuscript, Schlumberger Palo Alto Research Center, June 1988.

[Pearl, 1986] J. Pearl. Fusion, propagation, and structuring in belief networks. *Artificial Intelligence*, 29(3):241–288, September 1986.

[Pearl, 1987a] Judea Pearl. Distributed revision of composite beliefs. *Artificial Intelligence*, 33(2):173–215, October 1987.

[Pearl, 1987b] Judea Pearl. Probabilistic semantics for inheritance hierarchies with exceptions. Technical Report CSD-8700XX R-93-I, UCLA, Computer Science Department, Las Angeles, CA 90024-1596, July 1987.

[Peterson and Anderson, 1987] C. Peterson and James R. Anderson. A mean field theory learning algorithm for neural networks. Technical Report EI-259-87, MCC, August 1987.

[Pigman, 1984] Victoria Pigman. Krypton: Description of an implementation. Master's thesis, Stanford University, November 1984.

[Pollack, 1988] Jordan Pollack. Recursive auto-associative memory: Devising compositional distributed representations. Technical Report MCCS-88-124, Computing Research Laboratory, New Mexico State University, April 1988.

[Pylyshyn, 1984] Zenon W. Pylyshyn. Why "computing" requires symbols. In *Proceedings of the Sixth Annual Conference of the Cognitive Science Society*, pages 71–73, Boulder, Colorado, 1984.

[Quillian, 1968] M. R. Quillian. Semantic memory. In Marvin L. Minsky, editor, *Semantic information processing*, pages 227–270. MIT Press, Cambridge, Mass, 1968.

[Regier, 1988] Terry Regier. Recognizing image-schemas using programmable networks. In David S. Touretzky, Geoffrey E. Hinton, and Terrence J. Sejnowski, editors, *Proceedings of the 1988 Connectionist Models Summer School*. Morgan Kaufmann, 1988.

163

[Reiter, 1980] Raymond Reiter. A logic for default reasoning. *Artificial Intelligence*, 13:81–132, 1980.

[Rivest, 1988] Ronald L. Rivest. Game tree searching by min/max approximation. *Artificial Intelligence*, 34:77–96, 1988.

[Rumelhart *et al.*, 1986a] David E. Rumelhart, Geoffrey E. Hinton, and R. J. Williams. Learning internal representations by error propagation. In David E. Rumelhart, James L. McClelland, and the PDP research group, editors, *Parallel distributed processing: Explorations in the microstructure of cognition*, volume I, chapter 8, pages 318–364. Bradford Books, Cambridge, MA, 1986.

[Rumelhart *et al.*, 1986b] David E. Rumelhart, James L. McClelland, and the PDP research group. *Parallel distributed processing: Explorations in the microstructure of cognition. Volume I.* Bradford Books, Cambridge, MA, 1986.

[Rumelhart, 1986] David E. Rumelhart. Learning ISA hierarchies in a connectionist network. Talk given at the 1986 Connectionist Summer School, Carnegie-Mellon University., June 1986.

[Schank, 1982] Roger C. Schank. *Dynamic memory: a theory of reminding and learning in computers and people.* Cambridge University Press, Cambridge [Cambridgeshire] : New York, 1982.

[Schmolze, 1985] James G. Schmolze. The language and semantics of NIKL. Unpublished manuscript, Bolt Beranek and Newman Inc., April 1985.

[Schrödinger, 1946] Erwin Schrödinger. *Statistical Thermodynamics.* Cambridge University Press, London, 1946.

[Selman, 1987] Bart Selman. Analogues. Unpublished manuscript, University of Toronto, March 1987.

[Shastri, 1987] Lokendra Shastri. *Semantic Networks: An Evidential Formulation and its connectionist realization.* Morgan Kaufmann, Los Altos, CA, and Pitman, London, 1987.

[Shortliffe, 1976] Edward H. Shortliffe. *Computer-based medical consultations, MYCIN.* Elsevier, New York, 1976.

[Simon, 1981] Herbert A. Simon. *The Sciences of the Artificial*. MIT Press, Cambridge, Massachusetts, 1981.

[Touretzky and Geva, 1987] David S. Touretzky and Shai Geva. A distributed connectionist representation for concept structures. In *Proceedings of the Ninth Annual Conference of the Cognitive Science Society*, pages 155–164, Seattle, Washington, 1987.

[Touretzky and Hinton, 1985] David S. Touretzky and Geoffrey E. Hinton. Symbols among the neurons: Details of a connectionist inference architecture. In *Proceedings of the Ninth International Joint Conference on Artificial Intelligence*, pages 238–243, Los Angeles, California, 1985.

[Touretzky et al., 1987] David S. Touretzky, John Horty, and Richmond Thomason. A clash of intuitions: the current state of non-monotonic multiple inheritance systems. In *Proceedings of the Tenth International Joint Conference on Artificial Intelligence*, pages 476–482, Milan, Italy, 1987.

[Touretzky, 1986a] David S. Touretzky. BoltzCONS: Reconciling connectionism with the recursive nature of stacks and trees. In *Proceedings of Eighth Annual Conference of the Cognitive Science Society*, pages 522–530, Amherst, MA, 1986.

[Touretzky, 1986b] David S. Touretzky. *The Mathematics of Inheritance Systems*. Pitman, London, 1986.

[Tversky and Kahneman, 1982] Amos Tversky and Daniel Kahneman. Judgements of and by representativeness. In Daniel Kahneman, Paul Slovic, and Amos Tversky, editors, *Judgement Under Uncertainty: Heuristics and Biases*, pages 84–98. Cambridge University Press, 1982.

[Vilain, 1985] Marc B. Vilain. The restricted language architecture of a hybrid representation system. In *Proceedings of the Ninth International Joint Conference on Artificial Intelligence*, pages 547–551, Los Angeles, California, August 1985.

[White, 1984] Steve R. White. Concepts of scale in simulated annealing. Unpublished paper presented at the 1984 Simulated Annealing Workshop, IBM TJ Watson Research Center, Yorktown Heights, NY, April 1984.

[Willshaw, 1981] David Willshaw. Holography, associative memory, and inductive generalization. In Geoffrey E. Hinton and J. A. Anderson, editors, *Parallel models of associative memory*, chapter 3, pages 83–104. Erlbaum, Hillsdale, NJ, 1981.

[Woods, 1975] William A. Woods. What's in a link: Foundations for semantic networks. In Daniel G. Bobrow and Allan M. Collins, editors, *Representation and Understanding: Studies in Cognitive Science*, pages 35–82. Academic Press, New York, 1975.

[Zadeh, 1986] Lofti A. Zadeh. Test-score semantics as a basis for a computational approach to the representation of meaning. *Literary and Linguistic Computing*, 1(1):24–35, July 1986.